M000209264

Breaking Into Prison

How God Used One Ordinary Guy
to Get the Gospel to Millions

Prison Book Project
PO Box 592
Titusville, FL 32781

David Howell

Support This Ministry

Prison Evangelism, Inc., has distributed the gospel book *How to be a Child of God* free to 2,100 prison units throughout the United States representing more than 2 million captives. Recently we have increased the size of our database to include most county jails as well as detainees held in ICE units. Altogether we are able to reach some 12 million incarcerated men and women in 3,500 units across America. Our purpose is to *Change Hearts and Close Prisons.* This is accomplished by trusting and love in Jesus Christ. Without a change of heart, 70 percent will return to captivity within five years.

Help us set the captives free permanently by giving your financial support.

You can buy books for your own ministry at: **howtobeachildofgod.com**
All profits will buy more books for prisons and jails.

You can donate directly to this ministry at: **prisonevangelism.com**

Facebook: @ Prison Evangelism, Inc. and @ How to be a child of God

You can also mail a check to: **Prison Evangelism, Inc.**
P.O. Box 571977
Houston, Texas 77257

Prison Evangelism, Inc. is a 501c3 corporation.

As you read through this book and the accompanying copy of *How to be a child of God* in the back of this volume, think about how you can be an instrument for God to carry the message to the lost. To have the addresses of 12 million mostly lost souls is a great opportunity and a gift from God. They are the fruit, waiting to be harvested. All of us who have received the love and forgiveness of Christ have an obligation to carry His message to those who have not.

Example: A typical prison unit has approximately 1,000 beds. We know that one-third of these are open to receiving a gospel message. So we send at least 300 copies of *How to be a child of God* to that unit. Our cost is $162 or $.54 per copy delivered. Would you sponsor one unit for $162? More than likely, you would be participating in the salvation of more than 30 men and women!

Send $162 today and know that 30 are being saved.

Breaking Into Prison

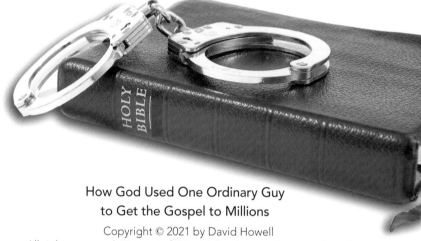

How God Used One Ordinary Guy
to Get the Gospel to Millions

Copyright © 2021 by David Howell
All rights reserved. No part of this publication may be reproduced
in any form without written permission from David Howell.

This title may be purchased in bulk for educational and
evangelical purposes. Please contact the publisher for more
information:

David Howell
P O Box 571977, Houston, Texas 77257
prisonevangelism.com
davidhowell@aol.com
info@HowtoBeaChildofGod.com
www.HowtoBeaChildofGod.com

Unless otherwise indicated, all Scripture quotations are taken
from the Holy Bible, New Living Translation,
copyright © 1996, 2004, 2007 by Tyndale House Foundation.
Used by permission of Tyndale House Publishers, Inc.,
Carol Stream, Illinois 60188. All rights reserved.

ISBN: 978-0-578-92355-0

Art direction and book graphic design by
John Magee, Houston, Texas • JohnMageeDesign.com

All illustrations by Randy Rodgers,
The Woodlands, Texas • artistguy@att.net

CONTENTS

A NOTE TO READERS

As you get into *Breaking Into Prison,* you will notice that the book's chapters, for the most part, alternate between (1) my personal story of how God worked through many decades in preparing me to reach millions of people in prisons with the gospel, and (2) a description of how the book ministry took flight and has looked in practice, as well as a couple of theological chapters that provide the underpinning of the ministry.

There is a reason for this arrangement. If I had arranged all the chapters chronologically, then this book would have looked like an autobiography with some chapters at the end about a prison ministry. But that is *not* what this book is about, so I didn't arrange it that way!

Rather, as I say right at the beginning of chapter 1, this book is a story about God—how out of His great love He wanted to get the good news of Jesus Christ into the hands of millions of people in U.S. jails and prisons, and how He prepared and used someone (in this case, me, but it could have been anyone!) to accomplish that task. And He did it through a simple little booklet called *How to Be a Child of God,* which has been added to the latter portion of this book.

It wasn't until the last decade (my 8th) that I even realized all that He was doing. But He knew all along.

It is my prayer that every reader of this book goes away with a deeper personal, practical understanding of what Paul laid out in Galatians 2:20:

> *I have been crucified with Christ; and it is no longer I who live, but Christ lives in me; and the life which I now live in the flesh I live by faith in the Son of God, who loved me and gave Himself up for me.*

It's not I who live, but Christ lives in me. Praise God. Because truly only He could have ever accomplished all of this.

David Howell
Houston, Texas
August 2021

Chapter 1

A Story About God

Christ in You
Colossians 1:27

This isn't a story about me. It's a story about God. It's a story about what God always seems to do: take an ordinary person and use them to accomplish extraordinary things for His kingdom. In this case, I was the ordinary person. About as ordinary as you can get. Maybe a little less than ordinary!

God could have chosen and equipped anyone. That's what He does, all the time.

Really, this is a story about how Jesus Christ lives through His Body us on earth. How Christ comes to live in us when we place our trust in Him. How He lives through us when we make ourselves available to Him surrender as His vessels. How He prepares us, sometimes over the course of an entire lifetime, to accomplish exactly the work He has prepared for us to do.

What was the work God prepared for me? To get the good news of Jesus Christ into the hands of millions of men and women prisoners in America through the booklet He wrote through me, *How to Be a Child of God.*

What was the raw material God had to work with? A profane South Texas rebel who started working in the oilfields at 14, lost his virginity in a Mexican whorehouse, became a drunkard and a druggie by age 18, was thrown in jail repeatedly into his 30s, married four times, and fathered a child by a fifth woman. That's really *raw material.*

An Illustration from How to Be a Child of God.

Only God could make it happen.

This is that story. It's not really a story about me. It's a story about the grace, kindness, and patience of a loving heavenly Father, and about Jesus, who, according to the Father's plan, came to live in me, and through me to reach millions with the life-changing gospel.

God took a long time to make it all happen. He's never in a hurry.

How did God do it? You don't just wake up one day and say, "I think I'd like to get the gospel into the hands of several million people who, more than any other group, are at the end of their rope and will be more open than anyone to the good news of Jesus." Well, you can wake up and say that if you like. But to actually accomplish it takes preparation. In my case, about seventy years of preparation.

All along, I had no idea what God was doing. I was like that tapestry that people like to use as an illustration of our lives. My life seemed like a jumble of unrelated rabbit trails, misadventures, poor choices, career successes and failures, and encounters with God (in the second half of my life, anyway). In my 40s, 50s, and 60s, I could tell God was at work, but toward what end I had no idea. It was all like the back side of a woven tapestry. A disconnected mess.

Then one day God flipped the tapestry around, and WOW! Look what you've been doing all along, God!

I've discovered that God doesn't waste anything. Even through all my many failures, God was shaping me to be the exact vessel He wanted to live through, to reach an unwanted and forgotten group of people whom He loves. They are men and women much like the "sinners and tax collectors" that Jesus hung around with on earth. They are men and women that Jesus died for. And that He wanted to bring a message of life to. The message of abundant life.

So, if the good work God has prepared for you is getting the good news of Jesus into the hands of millions of prisoners, how do you equip yourself for the task?

You don't. God does the equipping.

It helps to be able to relate to what it's like being in prison. God took care of that. Well, I took care of that myself, and God graciously used it.

It helps to know what it's like to succumb to drug and alcohol addiction, as so many prisoners have. Ditto on that one. (I estimate that 70% of men and 90% of women are incarcerated for drug- and alcohol-related issues, incidents or behavior.)

It helps to know how to relate well to people who aren't particularly sophisticated. I started out working as a roughneck on oil and gas drilling rigs.

It helps to be experienced in mass mail marketing. God took care of that.

It helps to know how to get material professionally printed and published. God took care of that, too.

It helps to be trained as an evangelist, and to communicate in simple ways that a fifth grader (the average inmate's education) can understand. God did that.

It helps to have encountered God in such a life-changing way that you can honestly say to people, "God radically changed me, and He can change your life, too." God did that. And in a big way.

It helps to have a message to offer people more than just "Jesus died for your sins, and if you believe in Him, you, too, can go to heaven." That's a wonderful message, to be sure, but prisoners need something that will change their lives now, not just in the sweet by and by. God gave me that message, and made it real in my own life.

Finally, it helps to live long enough for God to somehow make all of this come together. Now that was a miracle. In sum, it took God seventy years of equipping and training.

But it didn't start pretty.

1.1 million
This is how many books that have been sent into U.S. prisons and jails (as of December 2020)

Over 5 million
This is how many people we can estimate have read the books

Over 100,000
This is a conservative estimate of how many souls have been added to God's kingdom

This is the 50-page book that God used me to produce. This booklet is also produced in full in the back of this volume as reference.

Chapter 2

My Story:
What God Had to Work With

If you're going to know how to relate to prisoners, to get inside their heads, to know how they think and what their deepest needs are and how to communicate with them, it helps to grow up around some rough people. Or be a rough person. Or spend time behind bars yourself.

I did all three.

That's where this story about God began.

I grew up in an oilfield family in Alice, Texas. Alice is 45 miles west of Corpus Christi. If it's not the middle of nowhere, you can certainly see the middle of nowhere from there. About 8,000 people lived in Alice when I was born.

My folks actually did well financially. My dad was a drilling contractor and operated several drilling rigs. He drilled wells both for others and also on his own, and ended up selling his oil interests to a company for a good amount, but then he went bankrupt when I was eighteen. As a kid I rode with my dad when he went to drilling sites or called on investors in Houston, San Antonio, or Corpus Christi. We called on George Mitchell, father of the oil shale boom and future billionaire, as well as Oscar Wyatt, a great innovator in natural gas markets. I was enthusiastic to learn about the oil business.

Dad convinced me that I could do anything I could dream of. In the natural realm that "I can do it" attitude helped me achieve a certain level of success. In the spiritual realm, it stunted me. God had to teach me that I really couldn't do it, that in reality I was completely dependent on Him.

I look back and see all the times God was calling me and I never knew it. It's clear, in retrospect, that He had His hand on me all along, despite all of my efforts to the contrary.

Our family went to the Methodist church in town. I wasn't all that interested. Every week my brother and sister got a weekly mailer from the church.

One day I asked my mom, "Why am I the only one who doesn't get one of those?"

"Because everyone else has joined the church, but you haven't." That was news to me. "You have to make a decision and become a member."

I decided to pass. At age 13, other things held considerably more appeal. My dad had said to me, "David, you're bigger than I was when I went to work in the oilfield. You need to go to work."

I thought that was a great idea (and there were no laws at the time against a 13-year-old doing so). I started working on one of his rigs and making grown-up money, more than I knew how to spend. I loved it. I loved the independence that it gave me, and it put me light-years ahead of anyone I knew in starting a career. Because of that training I was always able to make a living in the oilfield.

Unfortunately, it also catapulted me light-years forward into a life focused on destructive self-indulgence.

When I was still 13 about ten of us boys brought bottles of rum and vodka and tequila out to a ranch and got drunk. Nine of the ten got sick, started throwing up, and swore they would never do that again. One of the ten thought it was the greatest thing ever. That was me. I loved the way it made me feel. I was already on the road to being an alcoholic.

Once I began working in the oilfield, I started running around with the guys on the rig, all older than me, of course. We would drive 90 miles south to Mexico, get drunk, and go to Mexican whorehouses. I was 14.

Soon, most of my life revolved around drinking. I didn't smoke marijuana in those days, but I did pop diet pills and prescription speed which were readily available in Mexico. I didn't care about anything but my own desires. Total selfishness ruled. Unfortunately, the teen years are when you really start to learn a lot of life lessons. Most of my lessons, however, were tainted with whiskey or the various drugs I was taking. Liquor became the center of my life. Sex was not far behind.

The sad thing is that when I started using alcohol and drugs my childhood was effectively over. In addition, my reputation of being wild, and running with a wild, mostly older crowd cost me a lot of possible friends and girlfriends in junior high and high school, and any lessons that a nicer, saner, more focused group might have offered.

God had me on a leash, though. A long one, for sure, but He still had me.

My dad didn't go to church himself when I was growing up, but he did believe that church and faith were important, so he encouraged me to go. Starting when I was 13, Dad enticed me by letting me take his car to Methodist Youth Fellowship on Sunday nights. I went to church camps, too, but I don't ever remember being confronted about salvation, the need to have a real relationship with Christ. Maybe I just wasn't open to hearing it, though.

Sometimes in my teens I would go to the Baptist church because their girls were prettier. Some of the parents insisted that if you wanted to spend time with their daughters, you had to meet them at church. That was a small price to pay!

The one thing that kept me in the loop with some of the nicer crowd in Alice was the fact that my dad had some money. We were well off financially. In my mind, I was able to live in two worlds: one where I could indulge my addictions and fleshly desires and one where I could be a more respected member of the community because my dad had some money and influence. I was learning to deceive myself as much as I tried to deceive others.

About this time, some friends and I were caught breaking into an ice house to steal some beer. I was old enough to be sent to state reform school. My dad had to pull a lot of strings to stop that from happening. I was starting to learn what money could solve, and that using influence and using friends could open doors.

My parents finally had enough of my bad behavior. When I was still 14, they sent me to Allen Military Academy in Bryan, Texas (near Texas A&M). For me, it was another adventure to savor. The adventure was short-lived, however. A friend and I got caught burglarizing some houses and I was kicked out of school in December of my first semester.

Come January, I was at Kemper Military School in Booneville, Missouri. It was an honor school, sanctioned by the U.S. Army. You could earn a regular Army PFC stripe just by graduating from high school there. Academics came easily for me and I did things right long enough to last there a couple of years.

Not that I didn't deserve to be kicked out. Three friends and I took some practice rifles, 22s, out of the armory one day and played war around campus during our time off. We were using live ammunition and one of us got shot in the chest. He walked around with a bullet in him for two days before turning himself in at the infirmary. Somehow, the whole thing was swept under the rug and I didn't get into trouble.

While I was at Kemper, my sister Anne was a freshman at Stephens College, twenty miles down the road. Our parents had let her take a car up there, which we and our friends used to go to bars in neighboring towns that let us drink after hours. We would grab our fake IDs, sneak down the fire escape after lights out, go drink, and make it back before daylight.

One fateful night I got caught. They kicked me out of Kemper. Same old story. I thought I was bulletproof and couldn't get caught. I always did eventually. At any of these crossroads, I could have done the right thing and my life would have been totally altered. If I had stayed out of major trouble at Kemper and graduated, I could have gone to college at almost any school in the country, even Yale. But God was always willing to use the path that I did choose.

The truth is that alcohol and drugs—mostly alcohol—were increasingly ruling my life. I lived a crappy life in a mental and emotional fog. They say a person stops maturing emotionally when he starts additively drinking or drugging. Using those criteria, I spent 28 years being a fourteen-year-old, until age 41 when I sobered up. Alcohol and drug addiction take away a person's dignity, his ability to reason, have healthy emotions, or love, and the capacity

As a child of our parents with a family lineage going back to Adam, we died spiritually with Adam in the Garden of Eden.

We carry the burdens of that lineage, plus the burdens of our own sins and the emotional baggage we pick up in our lifetime on earth. It is a real bag of junk with shame, guilt, past problems and hang-ups, and bad feelings about our sins and character defects. We are in need of a new lineage and a new family.

7   Romans 3:23, Romans 5:12, Romans 5:18a

An autobiography—of all of us.

to know the difference between right and wrong. After a while, an addictive personality ceases to have a conscience. It's a recipe for self-indulgence and hurting a lot of people.

I went back home to Alice and started entering youth rodeos as a bareback bronc and bull rider. Some of us riders used to pop diet pills (methamphetamine), thinking they gave us courage to ride 2000-pound bulls. I would get on one, wrap my rope in a suicide wrap, and yell "Release this beast!" I had to be totally insane. All of the props made me look like a serious rider, but I was only doing it for the parties and the girls. Many times I should have died or at least been seriously injured. But God protected me.

One night outside a dance hall near Robstown, Texas I had sex in the back of a car with a girl I had just met. I was 17; she was 15. I never saw her again, but I found out years later that she got pregnant and gave the baby up for adoption.

After I got into enough trouble again, my parents shipped me off to another military school, Schreiner Institute in Kerrville, Texas for my senior year. I almost made it to graduation before they expelled me for drinking and being absent without leave.

I moved back to Alice and started working on rigs again. It's funny, I remember driving to jobs in my new car and listening to gospel music on the radio. I didn't understand it much, and what they were singing about didn't sink in, but I just loved the sound. I would even listen to the preaching sometimes.

God kept drawing me to Him, letting the weight of my poor choices grow heavier, all the while preparing me for a new lineage and a new family.

Chapter 3

An Open Door to Prisons

Many decades later, God used all of my bad choices and misadventures for His good purposes. I was almost 70 when I started writing *How to Be a Child of God*. I didn't really know who I was writing it for. I had certain people in mind, of course, I still wanted something I could share with Alcoholics Anonymous (AA) people. But God knew exactly who *He* had in mind.

A young woman, whom I had asked to review the proof, came back to me and said, "I took a course in spiritual therapy from a guy who has a prison ministry in East Texas. His name is Paul Carlin. He used to be high up in Baptist circles, but he was sent to prison for securities fraud. After he got out, he started a prison ministry. Do you mind if I send him a copy of the booklet?"

(A side note: I have found that almost any time someone gets involved in prison ministry, it's legit. Let me tell you, there's no material reward in prison ministry!)

"Go ahead," I told her.

Four days later I got a call from Paul Carlin.

"I just got a copy of this booklet you produced," he said. "You need to get 100 copies of this book into every Texas prison. Today."

"How many prisons are there?" I asked him.

"114. I just emailed you all the addresses. You can send them straight to the chaplains. They will get them into prisoners' hands, I promise you."

This guy spoke with authority. I knew it was God. I would need almost 12,000 books to accomplish that task. My first printing was 15,000 books, so I would even have some left over. I shipped 100 books to each of 114 Texas prisons.

That was in 2012. From original idea to actually having books in hand, ready to send to people, had taken almost four years.

I still had no idea that God was calling me to prison ministry. I knew nothing about that kind of ministry, and I had certainly never given it any thought. I was just walking through a door that God had opened for the books.

Page 1

9-19-19

Dear, David

Hello, Mr. Howell.. My name is Randall, i have been incarcerated for 5 years now and have 4 more to go. First off I am 29 yrs. old, Born and raised in the Grand Canyon state, A-Z. Far up north toward the "four corners," in a place called THE NAVAJO Reservation. Where my tribe been since our release from fort Sumner. & So, That being said i've come to follow the word of God after the fact of coming from a Culture/Traditional background. For 4½ years now, i been growing in faith by reading the Bible. My Faith, and trust in God wont change, I Just Been having Trouble with understanding. Which I have prayed for, and then during that week of praying for more info, and Knowledge. Along Comes this Book, Because Every Two weeks on a Sunday they push a Bookcart →

Page 2

around for us to read. Just to make the picture more clear, im in the Hole/S·H·U housing Books. Not for getting in trouble, just of the simple fact that I've copporated with the Court prosecutors in my case. Which most prison yards Label a "Rat," anyway, thats besides the point. HOW TO BE A Child of God 'Came to me here, and for the first Time in my life, This Book has helped me better my self, in understanding. Spiritulally, Mentally and physically i've died and been raised up from my old self. By Jesus Christ and the holy spirt I finally See the way to salvation. By this Book that came to me after i prayed for more understanding, Is a miracle in it's self. God is Real, and now i know he really Sent his son To die for my sins. The purest white lamb, payed & Ultimate Sacrifice for me. And i come to understand with the realization that Your Book has showed+ Me.

A letter from an inmate

Texas Department of Criminal Justice
Institutional Division

·**Price Daniel Unit**

June 5, 2012

David Howell
How to be a Child of God
1535 West Loop South, Suite 200
Houston, Texas
77027

Dear Brothers and Sisters in Christ,

I want to thank you for all of the copies of *How to be a Child of God*! I put them out this weekend for Chapel services and they flew out the door. They were very well received. I know that materials like these are not cheap so please pass my thanks on those that helped provide them.

Keep up the good work and thank you for caring for those that so many have forgotten.

George Hanson

Chaplain George Hanson
Price Daniel Unit
938 South FM 1673
Snyder, TX 79549

325-573-1114

Within two weeks I started to get a clue. I had put my address in the front of the book, and letters started arriving. Handwritten letters from prisoners saying, *"This book has changed my life."*

Letters from chaplains saying, "I put out all the copies you sent for the inmates, and they flew off the shelf. I'm all out."

The letters are what God used to tell me that prisoners were His intended audience. I saw a huge need being met. Over and over, I would hear from prisoners:

"I never understood the Bible, but I understand this picture book."

"I don't understand King James, but I understand these words, the New Living Translation."

"I never really got this message until I looked through all of these pictures. Now I understand it."

Many of the letters would say something like, "I just finished *How to be a Child of God*. It's the first book I've ever read front to back."

One of those early handwritten letters, dated September 24, 2012, read:

Greetings and Respect to you Mr. David Howell. My name is _____. I'm doing a life sentence here in Beaumont for murder. The reason why I'm writing is your book How to be a Child of God is great and I would like more of your books. I have family of three, mom dad kids. I don't have anyone. I was wondering if you could find a Pen Pal.

I would read letters like that (even the parts that didn't always make complete sense!), and I would say to myself, "Wow! This is what I'm supposed to do."

Very quickly it became apparent that God had called me to do mass evangelism. I had always been taught that evangelism had to be done one on one. But Jesus frequently didn't do it one on one. He would speak to 5000 or more at a time. That was mass marketing back then. And I realized that that method of evangelism was not only okay, it was what God was calling me to. I would do mass marketing evangelism by mail. I would ship booklets to prisons. Chaplains would hand them out to inmates. Prisons are closed environments. The booklets would get read and passed around. Men's and women's lives would be changed.

Chapter 4

My Story:
God's Early Training

If God was going to prepare me to do the work He had chosen for me to do, He had to train me. He had already used my dad, of course, to give me a decent amount of training. From him I learned how to interact with people of influence, how to put together and sell deals, and how to be determined and persist no matter what the setbacks.

Now I needed some vocational training, so to speak. I needed to learn how to be a mass marketer.

Despite not having a high school diploma, I took some entrance tests and got into Texas A&I University (now Texas A&M—Kingsville). As a freshman I signed up for a credit course on the parables of Jesus and the next semester I took one on the Gospel of John. I may have been the only non-Bible thumper in those classes. Guys like me just didn't sign up for them, to say the least, but I was curious about God stuff. I even started going to the hymn-sing the Methodist church had on Wednesday nights for college kids. They would ask for song requests and I would request salvation songs with the invitations in them to surrender. What was going on in my mind? I don't know. He was definitely working on me while I thought I was satisfying my own intellectual curiosity. Maybe subconsciously I knew that, ultimately, I really did need to surrender to God.

I almost got expelled from Texas A&I for getting drunk and burning the homecoming bonfire a week before it was set to be burned. I flunked out, anyway. My mind was always on booze and drugs and women and making money, and it was hard to find time in the midst of all of that to study.

I started to bounce around from college to college. I tried a semester in junior college while working for an investment banking firm in Corpus Christi. Then I moved to New York, got my NASD license to buy and sell securities, and worked on the trading floor of an investment banking firm on Wall Street. And, as usual, I took some classes, this time at City College of New York. I was barely 21. Walking around town, I found a place called Union Square, an open area where a Salvation Army band would play. I used to walk down there to listen to them. Someone there tried to share the gospel with me one day, but I didn't want to talk about myself and where I

This is the same Jesus who died for all of our sins, faults, and character defects; past, present and future. Through His blood, we can be cleansed and made right before God. We can receive total forgiveness and unconditional love from God the Father. With His death and return to life, Jesus bridged the gap between God and man. That is why He is the Savior of the World.

John 3:16, I Peter 3:18, I Timothy 2:5-6, Romans 5:1   12

The message that I didn't yet understand.

stood with God. I was just there for the music, or so I thought. But God was knocking at my heart.

I finally realized that New York was not for me. After a little over a year I moved back to Texas, took some government courses at Kingsville, got involved in politics and campaigning, and started to make a bit of a name for myself in those circles. I loved it, and it started consuming me. Myself and some other students were setting up Young Republicans clubs in South Texas. We got so good at it that we successfully set up three clubs in a single day. To celebrate, one of my female co-workers, Mary Louise, and I got drunk and went to a motel in Alice and had intimate relations. Mary Louise was a genius. Literally. IQ of 159, with a photographic memory. She just wasn't that smart to get involved with me!

I decided to go crash the Republican state convention that year (1962) in Fort Worth. I met some political movers and shakers from Houston and they took me under their wing. So I moved to Houston to work for the statewide at-large congressional campaign of Desmond Barry. He lost the election, but for me the experience was invaluable. I was learning how to do advertising and marketing through a whole range of media: radio, TV, billboards, signs, and, of special note, direct mail. It was the direct mail training that would later be essential in how God wanted to use me.

At the same time I was doing campaign work, I was taking classes (again!), this time at the University of Houston. I was 22 and I figured I finally needed to get a degree, but I still wasn't serious enough about it. Chasing women, alcohol, politics, and making money appealed to me far more, and I flunked out again.

Shortly after I moved to Houston, Mary Louise called.

"I'm pregnant," she said.

I wanted to do the upright thing. "After the election in November," I told her, "I'll pick you up and we'll get married."

I was true to my word. We took a couple of friends with us across the border to Nuevo Laredo and married in a civil ceremony. We never lived together. I took her back to her hometown near Corpus Christi and I returned to my political work in Houston. After the baby was born the following spring, we got a divorce. Mary Louise married a childhood sweetheart and her husband asked to adopt the baby boy, so I gave up parental rights.

After the election, I stayed on with the same political team and started working on the campaign of Jim Bailey, running for mayor of Houston. I became his aide and driver. We would drive all over town to four or five speaking engagements a day. I learned a ton about retail politics and about raising money. I met a lot of rich folks and learned how to operate in that arena.

I also learned a lot about living life well (not that I was actually ready to do that). Jim taught a course through the local Catholic diocese about getting out of your self-focus, working with others, and doing things for others. All over town as we held meetings, people would come up to Jim, thanking him that this course had changed their lives. I got curious.

"What is this course that you've taught everyone?" I asked him.

"It's about taking individual responsibility and how it's better to light your own candle than curse the darkness."

I wanted to take it, but I wasn't Catholic, so I couldn't. But over the course of a couple of months of driving around together, Jim progressively taught it to me. I didn't even realize at the time that he was doing it. We were just talking. But it impacted me significantly. There was more to life, I began to realize, than living for yourself.

After the campaign (Jim lost), I wanted to start making good money in the oilfield equipment business. Since I had been learning how to do direct mail marketing, I figured that was the best way to go. A friend referred me to a direct mail marketing guru in Houston who for some reason was willing to teach me all he knew for free. For months he showed me how to construct a sales letter and sequence the materials and provide for a return response, and the metrics to measure the results. I started to implement what he had taught me.

In 1964, I got heavily involved with the Goldwater campaign in Texas. Through that work I further honed my skills in writing press releases and pamphlets and putting together marketing brochures.

In just a few short years, God had taught me how to run an advertising and marketing campaign, how to do direct mail marketing, how to hobnob with people of money and power, and how to raise money. I had no idea at the time, of course, that He was simply laying the groundwork, providing skills that decades later would be critical to the good works He prepared me to do since time began. At the time I thought I was simply enjoying politics and making money.

I had made friends in Houston and was part of a party scene. Sometimes, though, I would go places I was quite sure none of them went. Tent revivals happened from time to time on the east side of town. I would go out there and watch. I was intrigued by the whole operation, that they could draw such a crowd and get people to give money. I remember a faith healer doing his thing at one of them. It seemed like people were actually getting healed. I didn't understand much of what I heard out there, but maybe subconsciously I was wanting to hear or understand a message that I knew was for me. God kept calling me to Him.

I didn't go to any church regularly, but I did start dating this one woman that I went to church with. We would go to parties on Saturday nights, get drunk, have intimate relations, and then on Sunday morning I would say, "Let's go to church." There was a well-known pastor nearby that I liked to listen to. God was still tugging at my heart.

Chapter 5

Why the Book Struck a Chord

You might think that prisons would be swimming with Christian material. They aren't. Either the material isn't there at all, or it's not in a form that inmates can relate to. The typical prison inmate in America has the equivalent of a fifth-grade education. If he's curious about God, you can hand him a Bible and he'll start reading in Genesis with fifth-grade comprehension. How far do you think the average fifth grader would get reading the Pentateuch? How far do you think the average prisoner gets—if he's willing to open it at all?

Most Christian material isn't any more appealing. How many fifth graders are going to wade through a 250-page book on Christian living, to say nothing of Christian theology? Really, how many Christians of any age will read that kind of book anymore? Not many. If 10,000 copies of such a book are sold, that's a success!

There are exceptions to this rule sitting in prisons, of course, but for the most part, with this population, everything has to be kept simple. God is the expert at simple. What do we think Jesus's parables were? They were a way to communicate the truths of the kingdom of God to a simple audience. What did the Apostle Paul, an extensively educated man, say? "The Greeks can have all their great wisdom; I only know Christ and Him crucified" (see 1 Corinthians 2:2). What was the Incarnation? It was God saying to humanity, "If you want to know who I am, look at this Man." Jesus was the *exact* image, the picture, of God (Hebrews 1:3).

Why did *How to Be a Child of God* find such a receptive audience in prisons?

I think, first, it held their attention. The book had good pictures, and lots of them. I like books with pictures. Don't you? We never outgrow that. People with a fifth-grade education especially haven't outgrown that.

Second, it had large print. Many prisoners don't have the reading glasses they need. The book designers and printers kept telling me, "You need to use smaller print." I would tell them, "Not if I want the thing to be read, I don't!"

Third, it had simple words. Church people so easily lapse into theological jargon. Talking about redemption and sanctification doesn't mean anything to an immigrant from Mexico who didn't finish the second grade. "I came that they might have life," Jesus said (John 10:10). Most of us can understand that.

Fourth, it had a main character, so to speak, that prisoners could relate to. John Magee, a graphics designer in Houston, gave me the idea of this young guy in a baseball cap. He's the guy who carries through the entire story, who holds the whole thing together.

He is *Everyman*. He's just living his life, trying to make things work for himself, trying to make life match what he wants. He is living for himself, which is really all that sin is: living with ourselves as the center, being our own god.

Anyone can relate to him, because all of us are who he is. I can especially relate to him as he is pictured in the follow-up booklet (*Seeking God Through Prayer and Meditation*), walking on a tightrope over a canyon filled with all the things that want to destroy us, things like: lust, money, pride, etc. I thought I had the world by the tail, when it was actually God keeping me from falling completely into the pit of self-destruction, holding my hand across that tightrope. He intended to get me to the other side, even when I seemed intent on destroying myself. His angels were really guiding my steps.

That's the way it is for so many of us—all of us, really. It's certainly true of men and women in prison. Those of us outside of prison, who look like we've lived much more respectable lives outside of Christ, are just as self-destructive. We just don't know it. For many people, life hasn't gotten bad enough for them to realize the lifelessness of it all. Which is exactly the point! God has to bring us to the place where we realize we are missing the life. Then we are ready for the one who is the life.

The young man in the baseball cap doesn't know it for much of the booklet, but he is actually a conduit for what God wants to accomplish through him. He is a conduit for the life of Christ. He doesn't know it until he receives Christ, of course. And if he's like most Christians, he doesn't even know that afterward! But in the booklet God makes it a reality to him. He wants to make that a reality to all of us.

The speaker gives examples, illustrations, and stories to prove or bring to light a point, and he or she teaches the application we are to take to heart. When we meditate on a particular subject that is being taught or discussed through God's Word, we can implement His truth into our lives.

Listen carefully as God gives you life instructions through the spoken word as well as the written word. The Sermon on the Mount in Chapters 5-8 of the Book of Matthew is a wonderful design for living.

Jesus teaches on salt and life:

"You are the salt of the earth. But what good is salt if it has lost its flavor? Can you make it salty again? It will be thrown out and trampled underfoot as worthless. You are the light of the world—like a city on a hilltop that cannot be hidden. No one lights a lamp and then puts it under a basket. Instead, a lamp is placed on a stand, where it gives light to everyone in the house. In the same way, let your good deeds shine out for all to see, so that everyone will praise your heavenly Father." Matthew 5:13-16

38

The Everyman in the baseball cap

Chapter 6

My Story: A Rough Life That God Had His Hand On

At this point in my life God shifted gears and trained me in an entirely different realm. Humanly speaking, it looked like a detour, one big rabbit trail. It wasn't.

If God is going to prepare you to do prison ministry in America, He'd better teach you how to relate to multiple population groups. One of those is Hispanics, who constitute a high percentage of the U.S. prison population. It helps to grow up in a place with a heavy Hispanic influence. South Texas was certainly that. It also helps to speak some Spanish.

From ages 26 to 28 I went to live in Mexico. I have always had a soft spot for Mexican culture and the Mexican people. Maybe it was because I grew up listening to Mexican music on the radio in South Texas, or maybe it was talking to Vera, a Mexican housekeeper who worked a long time for my family. There's not much difference between the culture in South Texas and that in Northern Mexico, or at least not at that time. The Rio Grande was just a river running through the middle of the place.

I moved to Saltillo, not far from Monterrey, went to Spanish language school, learned how to play the accordion, immersed myself in the culture, and drank a lot. I fell in love with a beautiful Mexican girl and dreamed of marrying her. One day I woke up sober and sensible and realized that if I married her and took her back to South Texas, I probably would be taking her fourteen brothers and sisters as well.

I left the next day before it was too late and went to Mexico City, where I took some more courses. I probably logged 40 or so college hours in Spanish, Latin American history, etc. I even tried my hand at learning Nahuatl, the ancient language of the Aztecs. I figured that maybe it would help me relate to the Indigenistas if I started working in advertising and marketing down there. My landlady in Mexico City tried to convince me that, based on my mother's name, LaVella, I actually was Mexican. Which would have been fine with me. More and more, I felt a oneness with the Mexican people and culture.

Perspectives

Many have had close calls through-out their lives and wondered how they survived. They tried successfully and unsuccessfully to balance material things in their lives believing they were smart, lucky or indestructible. They never understood that God knew their hearts and had sent angels to protect them until the time they would make a decision for Him. Therefore, angels are only servants-who will inherit salvation. Hebrews 1:14 NLT. Even before he made the world, God loved us and chose us in Christ to be holy and without fault in his eyes. Ephesians 1:4 NLT. For everyone has sinned; we all fall short of God's glorious standard. Romans 3:23 NLT When we were utterly helpless, Christ came at just the right time and died for us sinners. Romans 5:6 NLT

91

My natural ways weren't working too well,
but God was still protecting me and preparing me.

Toward the end of my second year in Mexico, I went over to the coast, to Acapulco, to a house owned by Cantinflas, the famous Mexican movie star. A friend of mine from the States had rented it. I was drunk one night and doing stunts when I catapulted myself off the third story balcony. I broke my neck and also some ribs, which stuck in the lining of my heart (the pericardium). They flew me to Mexico City and then to Houston, where the world-famous heart surgeon, Denton Cooley, operated on me. My dad told my old drinking buddies in Alice that I wasn't going to make it. They drove to the hospital to pay their last respects and were there when I woke up. I was surprised! God and His angels kept rescuing me from myself.

Accidents and mishaps like this, caused by my drinking, eventually helped lead me to the end of myself, so to speak. What's amazing is that it took so many of them and so much destruction in my life. Our capacity to hold onto our idols, regardless of how much damage they do, is virtually boundless.

Was my time in Mexico simply a detour, wasted time? Hardly. God uses everything. Growing up in South Texas, I was used to relating to Hispanic people already. But living in Mexico itself moved that forward. It caused me to have a special love for the Mexican people, a special appreciation for their culture, and a much greater ability to speak Spanish. Why, decades later, was that important? Because God opened the doors for me to do prison ministry, both in the United States and in Latin America. Guess what ethnic group is heavily represented in American prisons? Again, one of my target audiences was readily available as U. S Immigration and Custom Enforcement (ICE) keeps a large segment of their detainees in jails and prisons throughout the country.

God knew exactly what He was doing during this time.

I stayed in the States after my heart surgery. I got back into the oilfield equipment business, doing some deals with my dad, which I had done off and on through my 20s. I also got back into politics, I knew and worked with a lot of people in politics, both office holders and influencers.

Hard to believe, looking back, but during the Nixon campaign for president in 1968, I was offered a job as his personal assistant. I turned it down due to my own insecurities. That, primarily, was due to my drinking, and also because I didn't really feel worthy. I was associating with all of these highly educated guys and I didn't even have a college degree. A guy named Dwight Chapin from UCLA took the job instead. When Nixon was speaking and someone would hand him a glass of water, that was Dwight. He later became Deputy Assistant to the President after the election and was later convicted of a 1972 campaign violation and served some prison time.

If I had moved to DC permanently, I would have probably become a big lobbyist or a White House official. I would have been picked up for DWI at some point and messed it all up. I probably would have been involved in Watergate and maybe gone to prison for it. God was protecting me from that, and keeping me on the track where He knew He would eventually use me. What a fascinating God we have!

So I never worked directly for the government, but I did have close ties with people in the White House. I worked with them on lobbying projects from time to time. For example, I was able to get a large amount of nickel released from the government stockpile that contributed to breaking the union strike against nickel mines. That strike was allowing Russian nickel to come here and capitalize on a huge price increase. I couldn't prove it, but there was a tie between unions, the Mob, and Russian (Communist) nickel producers. Anyway, the release in the US stockpile which I facilitated ended it. The price of nickel went from $7 per pound back to $1.50 and the strike was broken.

I didn't know it at the time, of course, but God had a reason for all of this. Even though I had turned down the White House job, I was learning to be at ease running in circles of people of influence. That, too, was a skill I would need much later on.

My mother died of ALS in 1970 when I was thirty. She was only 58. Soon afterward my dad became a Christian. He was about 65, and God had been working on him, too. He got involved with the church and also hosted a Bible study at his house. As it turned out, the only ones who came were women!

He came to Houston and we went to church. The pastor was talking about the need to make a decision for God. I remember the basic message but somehow it just didn't penetrate. It's not that I had a sense of consciously understanding the choice and saying no. It's almost as if I didn't realize the question was being directed at me at all. I just wasn't ready.

My dad himself had also struggled with alcoholism the latter part of his life, but he finally got off alcohol. Unfortunately, after my mother died, he started taking Valium, from an open prescription she had, and got addicted to it. He didn't even realize it.

Valium can make you paranoid, and my dad kept becoming convinced that he had cancer. He constantly had the doctors check on him. The final time, he was in the hospital in Alice and they did a biopsy, which, once more, was negative. The truth was, he was a perfectly healthy 74-year-old. He went off Valium in the hospital, though, and on the third day he lapsed into a coma from withdrawal that he never came out of. I'm convinced that his body went into withdrawal shock or seizure from not taking Valium, the drug he was addicted to. I had a friend who died that way as well, but the withdrawal resulted in a heart attack.

The last several years of Dad's life, I was down in Alice helping him out quite a bit. I'm grateful for the time we had together, and forever grateful that he gave his life to Jesus.

Soon after Dad became a believer and came to Houston to visit, an old drinking buddy of mine that I had known in military school, Tom Crocker, called me.

"God saved me," he said. "I've come to know Jesus."

"Great," I said. I was sincere. I thought it was great when someone did something spiritual or godly.

He told me how rotten he had been, and how coming to know God had given him the desire and ability to turn his life around. That was a puzzle to me. I always thought that, among my friends, Tom was the one who pretty much walked the straight and narrow. If he was such a sinner, what did that make me? But I wasn't ready to come to terms with that yet.

Tom and I kept up with each other, and when I was 33, he said he wanted to come see me. He drove down from Dallas and took me through the "Four Spiritual Laws" witnessing tract. I had been drinking heavily for many years at that point and the alcohol was taking its toll on me in every way. Tom could probably see that more clearly than I could. He thought I might be ready to receive Christ and turn away from that life, but I wasn't. I politely prayed the sinner's prayer with him, supposedly asking Jesus to come into my heart and life, but I didn't really understand what I was doing and I knew I didn't mean it in my heart. The Savior again was knocking on the door of my heart, but I didn't answer.

After we finished all our spiritual stuff, I got up and asked Tom, "Can I fix you a drink?"

My career continued on in two veins: politics and the oilfield pipe and equipment business. Politics was mostly an avocation, though at times I seemed more devoted to it than to anything. But oilfield pipe and equipment is where I made a living. I was a wholesaler. By the time I was in my early 30s I had a developed an industry magazine—a glorified brochure, really—and accumulated a database of 15,000 oilfield personnel all over the world that I could market to. Periodically I would send out the magazine to all 15,000 of them and business would flow in.

What I had learned early on in my campaign work about developing databases and marketing materials came in very handy. God was teaching me that direct mail marketing worked!

At age 32, I married my best friend, Linda Underwood, with whom I had worked in politics for years. Linda and I met on a blind date and I taught her about campaign politics. Over time, I mean. Not all on the first date! She became the Young Republican National Committee woman from Texas and went to Washington to be on staff of the National Young Republican organization. We worked together on the Nixon for president and Bill Clements for Texas governor campaigns. She even worked at the White House for several years.

Like me, Linda was an alcoholic who, also like me, eventually recovered. Not before we divorced after six years, though.

When I was 36, I got thrown in jail for the sixth and final time of my life. Always before it was for being drunk and disorderly. This time it was for smoking a joint. For some reason, I was the only guy the Venezuelan government granted a license to export oilfield drilling equipment out of the country. Everyone else could import; only I could export. I found out about a large inventory of equipment that a company in Tyler, Texas had in Venezuela that they were trying to get rid of. So I went down to Venezuela and bought all the equipment, planning to export it.

Unfortunately, I was still drinking heavily. I was already drunk when I checked into a suite at the Hilton in Caracas and then went down to the hotel bar. I had just lit up a joint when a Venezuelan federal agent put a gun to my head. He arrested me and threw me in jail. I called the American embassy and they got me a lawyer.

"It'll take $25,000 for you to bribe the judge and get out," he told me.

"$25,000?" I replied. "Forget that."

On the ninth day in jail, I was talking to a fellow inmate who spoke English. I told him my story.

"How long have you been in here?" he asked me.

"Nine days."

"You know, they'll only hold you here for ten. Then they send you up in the mountains to Santa Rosa. Nobody gets out of Santa Rosa for two or three years."

I called my lawyer. "I'll offer him $15,000."

They took it and I wrote them a check from my business account. The check was hot, but they didn't discover that until I had left the country. I haven't been back to Venezuela.

So I had to sell the oilfield equipment to some other people in Venezuela and after a six-month investment of my time, instead of making a million dollars, I didn't make a dime. Just one of the countless times I had to pay for my alcohol and drug addiction.

God used even that, though. Having been in a Latin American jail, I have more of a heart for those who are stuck there. Many years later, God opened the door for me to get the gospel in Spanish to many prisoners down there.

Chapter 7

God's Ministry Takes Off

When it became obvious what God wanted me to do with the *How to Be a Child of God* booklets, I jumped into the project with both feet. I had been involved in mass mail marketing off and on for fifty years. God had made sure I was well trained.

Essentially, God was giving me the mailing addresses of two million of the best candidates to be evangelized in the country—to someone who was both an evangelist and a mass mail marketer.

Nothing could have been simpler. So many of these people, at the end of their rope, are ready to not only put their trust in Christ, but totally surrender to Him. Life as they have tried to live it hasn't worked for them. They are ready to receive true life from the Savior.

And the two million figure only included permanent inmates. There are also twelve million transient, shorter-term inmates locked up annually, in county jails, They are all candidates for salvation and the knowledge of Jesus Christ living His life in them and expanding His kingdom through them. For anyone with a desire to see people come to know Jesus, this was and is an abundance of low-lying fruit, indeed! And we know exactly where they are!

I started compiling a database of prisons and prison chaplains in the U.S. (2,100 federal and state prisons and large county jails) and began mailing out the booklets. Chaplains were wonderfully receptive to them. Not surprisingly, they loved having something to give inmates that the inmates actually enjoyed reading.

From: John Salmon
Subject: *HOW TO BE A CHILD OF GOD* Booklet
Date: November 17, 2013
To: "info@HowToBeaChildofGod.com"

Mr. Howell,
In the past we have received copies of your booklet,
HOW TO BE A CHILD OF GOD, free of charge to
be given to our offenders here at Diboll Correctional
Center. We exhausted our supply long ago and I am
writing to inquire about the possibility of restocking
our supply.

The booklets are very popular with the men. They
actually read it. And you know what happens when
people expose themselves to the Word of God.

Thanks for all you do,
Chaplain John Salmon
Diboll Correctional Center
1604 South First Street
Diboll, TX 75941

One prison chaplain in Iowa stopped being a chaplain and started a church as pastor. He wanted a bunch of copies of the book for his church, because he said he saw how it totally changed people inside the prison.

The more prisons I sent the booklets to, the more handwritten letters poured in.

As a whole, the letters told me several things. First, the booklets were getting passed around. They weren't getting grabbed up by single inmates and hoarded. An inmate would pick one up, read it, and pass it along to someone else. Based on the feedback I was getting (from both inmates and chaplains), I estimated that each booklet was being read by at least five inmates. Some would say ten. I had intentionally produced a sturdy book that would last, perfect-bound without staples (which most prisons won't allow, so they won't be turned into tattoo needles) and on heavy paper stock. I have found that the books have at least a three-year life. There is a tear out and coded reply card in the back of each book and we continue to receive these cards even after three years from the time distributed

Second, inmates weren't just reading them once. They were reading them multiple times. Something about the booklet and its message struck a chord with so many of them, and they kept rereading it to let its message sink in.

Third, God was bearing much fruit. Men and women were coming to Christ. Lives were being changed. They were telling me in the letters.

10-8-16

To Whom it may concern:

I want to dig a little deeper.
Please send me a free copy of
"SeeKING GoD THROUGH
PRAYER And MEDITATION

NAME: ███████████████
ADDress: ███████████████

NEWport, AR. 72112.

And what I think about your
Book: "How to be A child of God".

When I read this book the faith
God Allowed me to have through this
book was, Awesome, and I want
to pass this faith on to others,
So I Started to day to try the
lesson it officer offers in the
bACK. To pray for 10 people for
21 dAys. I am excited to see
God, move And SAve or plant A
Seed through me to others.

If you have A Bible
I need one of my own.

Page one of a letter from an inmate in prison in Arkansas.

I'm in Prison, And doing my
Best to Change my way of
thinking So I can Live a different
Kind Of Life. expecilly Knowing
how close Jesus really is, by
Your Child of God Book I Just
finish Showed me In Such plain
words how Close Jesus is with
me and I want to thank you
for following What the Lord lead
you to do because this book
has Changed my Life.

Thank you

Another letter from an inmate in Arizona State Correctional Facility.

To whom it may concern:

I N▓▓▓▓, ▓▓▓, z'am currently resided in Arizona state Department of Correction.
my last cell mate handed me a book before he went home it was entitled, "How to be a child of God".

This book has open my heart, mind, eye, and soul, And planty of unbeliveable passages.

I know understand lil more about with it is z want to do in life or my life z should say when z get out next year.

I've also been reading or begand reading a Bible, I enjoy it every moring the best when it the quiet, and z can talk with almightly lord about what ever come to heart.

This has also helped me to communicate with friends, family I've not in so so long.

Even my baby boy whom now a teen, that I've not spoke or wrote, or heared from in eleven year's. Thank you lord!

May you pleuse send a copy of "Seeking God through prayer's and meditation. If you have any other free book's or paplet's may you send them as well. Thank you very much, and you all have a very bless year,

Chapter 8

My Story: A Different Life, But Not the Life

God had delivered me out of the Venezuelan jail, and I was still searching. Not long after my Venezuelan fiasco, an opportunity arose to acquire some oilfield equipment from a bankrupt American company in Israel. No one in the oil business wanted an Israeli stamp on their passport in those days, since most of them had to do business with the Arabs. But I gladly went. On a day off there, my Romanian-born agent took me on a personal tour of Jerusalem.

"Here's the route where Jesus carried His cross," he said. "Here's what remains of King Herod's temple." And so forth. I was strangely moved by the whole experience.

The odd fact that this opportunity had arisen in Israel was not lost on me, either. Why was I the one guy with the chance to go there and see what I saw, buy what I bought, and sell Israeli equipment to some Iranians, no less?

The whole Israel experience got me to seriously thinking. Why did three of the world's major religions all get started, at least in part, in this one location? I decided that when I got home, I would read through the Old Testament.

At this point it was starting to register with me that I wasn't accomplishing what I wanted to in life. My drinking had interfered with my social life, my personal life, and my career (I had lost a couple of deals because of it). I realized alcohol was the most important thing in my life and that it was taking a huge toll on me. I had been throwing my life away.

We cannot have peace when we are separated from God. The choices, the ones we make every day, are self-centered and keep us frustrated and separated from fellowship with God. We have a deep yearning for a peaceful union with our Heavenly Father, but we lack that spiritual connection. Our own best thinking and good intentions got us into this mess.

Ecclesiastes 3:11, Romans 6:16, Luke 1:78-79, John 16:33, Romans 5:1-2, Romans 8:6   10

My root problem: I was separated from God.

Not long after my trip to Venezuela, Bill Clements, running for governor of Texas, asked my wife Linda and me to run his campaign in the Houston area. After he won, Clements offered me a job in Austin as his chief legislative liaison. I turned it down.

"Why?" he asked me.

"Well, I have this drug charge in Venezuela hanging over me."

"Does anyone know about it?"

"If I took this job somebody would find out."

I said he didn't need that kind of baggage. God was protecting me again. Working full time around that crowd, I would have been the biggest drunk in Austin and likely would have killed someone while driving drunk.

About this time, Linda told me she wanted a divorce if I did not stop drinking. With my selfish, lop-sided insane way of thinking, I thought that that might be a good thing, but I wanted it to be on my terms if I were to get a divorce. An addictive personality has no compassion and no love for anyone but himself and his addiction. No one else matters. Total self-centeredness prevails!

I told her I would go to Alcoholics Anonymous that day, which I did. I continued to go from time to time, but I didn't care that much about it and I wasn't ready to quit drinking. I kept embarrassing both myself and those around me with my behavior.

I also started drinking at a couple of taverns, since I couldn't drink at home anymore. I met a girl named Lalla at one of them. She was ten years my junior and seemed to accept me just the way I was. We got into a relationship, Linda found out, and she filed for divorce. I think back to the people I hurt so badly and all I can do is thank God for His forgiveness.

A few months later Lalla and I got married. We were at a friend's house in Victoria and called a Justice of the Peace to come out and perform the wedding. He was drunk when He got there and we had to prompt him through the ceremony. The honeymoon, so to speak, didn't last too long. We fought all the time. Not long after we married, Lalla said, "If you don't sober up, I'm filing for divorce." That sounded familiar!

I started thinking, "Maybe she's right. Maybe I am an alcoholic." I wanted my life to change, but I didn't want to stop drinking completely. I was half in and half out.

I drifted in and out of AA for the first couple of years we were married. I would get three months of sobriety and my mind would clear and I would remember those horrible episodes where I treated myself and others so badly. I couldn't stand myself, so I would go pour whiskey down my throat or smoke pot. I smoked a lot of pot in those days.

I was really getting into self-loathing and I was thoroughly fed up with life. On one occasion, I locked Lalla out of our house (and kicked her mother out as well). I bought a case of brandy and got a kilo of some heavy-duty Maui weed. My intent was to drink myself to death or bottom out and begin life anew. I was getting sick and tired of being sick and tired.

I passed out, but when I woke up, I saw that I had only drunk a small part of one bottle of brandy. "I'm getting wet brain," I said to myself. When you have wet brain, you can get drunk on relatively little alcohol, and your brain is being damaged. I knew I was in deep trouble. I figured I could afford to lose most things, but I couldn't afford to lose my mind and my ability to make, steal, con, or borrow money.

God still had His hand on me. He was allowing me to go down a road where I saw the end result of a life of self-destruction. I was destroying both myself and those around me. Lalla, by the way, was pregnant with our first daughter, Samantha.

I stopped drinking alcohol and just smoked pot. I fell in love with it, just as I had with whiskey, and couldn't get enough of the stuff.

I was going to one AA meeting a week, on Saturday mornings. One Saturday I rushed out at the end of the meeting, as usual, but this time three of my friends there followed me to my car.

"Why are you so angry?" one of them asked. "You always run out at the end of meetings and never say a word and you look so mad."

I told them that I really came to the meetings to show them I could stay sober without them. And then I laid it on the table. "After I leave here I go home and blast pot all week."

That was my moment of truth. As I shared the raw truth with these three fellow addicts and alcoholics, the weight of the lies that I carried was lifted off of me. I will never forget the relief I felt at that moment when I finally got honest with myself. I discovered later why I felt such relief. I had the capacity to be honest, and therefore I might have the capacity to get well. Looking back, that was my point of surrender—to my addiction, at least.

Even though I did not know God at that time, He knew me and I realized He was there. I still didn't know in what form or fashion, but nevertheless a supernatural power was by my side. I was satisfied with that at the time.

Two days later I met the same guys for lunch. They told me they had arranged for me to go to treatment at the famous Hazelden clinic in Minnesota. I simply responded, "When do I leave?"

At last, I had become teachable. I was ready to do what I was told and quit relying on myself for sobriety and everything else. Quite possibly, I was on the road to recovery from this horrible disease of addiction. God provided the money.

On the day of my flight, I missed the plane by a few minutes. It was an honest miscalculation. I asked for any plane going north, caught a flight to Chicago, and took a bus to Minneapolis. I was serious this time.

Hazelden helped me finally get over the hump and completely sober up. There was a lot of God talk at Hazelden. The counselor kept trying to teach me to breathe in God. I had no idea what he meant, but I tried. More and more, I was thinking about God and His role in all of this. I was even asked to pray over meals for the group there, which felt a bit awkward, but I quickly got into it.

I came back from Hazelden sober, and it stuck. I stayed sober. I spent the next two years working AA diligently, doing twelve-step work, helping to start new meetings, sponsoring new people, learning how to live. I learned to share what was going on with me, become more sensitive, softer hearted, honest and willing to learn. Somewhat.

After two years of being sober, I wasn't exactly having a lot of fun, at least not like I had envisioned it. I certainly wasn't enjoying life. I thought, "If this is all there is to being sober, I'd rather have my whiskey back." I was a good AAer, but there was a missing part somewhere.

What was God doing? I think He was showing me that someone simply cleaning his life up wasn't sufficient. He may be clean of alcohol, or drugs, or whatever, but he is still dead to God.

That's how God says we are all born into this world—dead to Him (Ephesians 2:1). We are created to be joined to God in the deepest part of our being, our spirit (1 Corinthians 6:17). We are meant to commune with Him there, relate to Him there, hear His voice there, be one with Him there. But we are born into the world with a spirit dead to God, unconnected to Him, unresponsive to Him. Our spirit has not yet been made alive.

Only the Holy Spirit can birth within us a new spirit, alive to God, and then join Himself to it. That's what it means to be born again. Being born again isn't gaining a new perspective on life, so that it seems like we've been born anew. Being born again is an actual event. The Holy Spirit births within us a new spirit, and then He comes inside us and joins Himself permanently to our new spirit. Jesus said that we must be born again. It's not optional. Only He can bring life to our deepest being. Jesus said He was the Life. If we don't have Him in our inmost being, we don't have Life. We aren't joined to God (Ezekiel 36:26-27; John 3:3-5).

I wasn't yet joined to God, and I knew something was missing. There had to be more.

> We attempt to bridge the gap that separates us from God, and we seek ways to reestablish a relationship with Him. None work. Only through trust in Jesus Christ can we get in touch with God the Father.

> Good Works
> Religion
> Money
> Morality

11   Proverbs 14:12, Romans 6:23, Romans 3:23

Getting sober was an improvement, but I still didn't have God's life.

Chapter 9

The Perfect Craftsman

What's amazing to me is how God used all of these different aspects of my life to prepare me for the work He ultimately had for me to do, even before I personally knew Him. Perhaps I shouldn't be so surprised. It's not like I'm the first one God has done this with. Hardly.

God is at work, preparing and equipping us both before and after we come to faith in Christ. He doesn't waste anything. He knows exactly what He intends to accomplish. He has prepared beforehand good works for each one of us to do.

> For we are His workmanship, created in Christ Jesus for good works, which God prepared beforehand, that we should walk in them. (Ephesians 2:10)

He is, in truth, the perfect craftsman.

So we are all meant to do good works, but everyone isn't meant to do the same good works. That's why we are God's workmanship. He has to prepare us specifically to do the work He has created us—recreated us in Christ, actually—to do.

God has prepared one person to do X, another person to do Y, and another person to do Z. He has formed one person to teach others to pray well. He's formed another to preach. He's formed another to share His love with toddlers. If the person sharing His love with toddlers says to himself, "This isn't of much value to God; I really ought to be doing something more for Him," he's missing it. God doesn't value X more than He values Y. He wants to accomplish both. And He's preparing different individuals to accomplish them.

Paul talked about this to the Corinthians. Basically, he said, "Look, everyone can't be the glamorous parts of the body. Some people have to be the unglamorous parts. God values both just as highly. So be what God has assigned you to be. Don't feel like you have to be what you aren't. And don't look down on others for being what God has made them to be" (see 1 Corinthians 12:18-23).

The Scriptures are full of examples of this. The man Jesus healed who was full of demons, for instance—the guy in the rock tombs who was cutting himself. Jesus healed him, and he said to Jesus, "Let me come with you; I want to be one of the people who follows you around." After all, that's what all the disciples were getting to do. But Jesus said, "No, here's what God has prepared you for: go back to your people and tell them what great things God has done for you." God prepared him for a specific good work (see Mark 5:18-20).

Probably the best example of this in the New Testament is the Apostle Paul. Paul said that God "set me apart before I was born" for the work He wanted him to do (Galatians 1:15-16). But God had to take him on a specific path to get him ready to be the apostle to the Gentiles and to write much of the New Testament.

What was that path? He was trained from childhood to be a Pharisee under the tutelage of the famous teacher Gamaliel (Acts 22:3). He was, by his own admission, blameless as far as righteousness according to the law (Philippians 3:6). He was so zealous for the law that he persecuted Christians, dragging them out of their houses and throwing them into prison (Acts 8:3). He was part of the group that murdered Stephen. After that, he was on his way to Damascus to arrest more believers (Acts 9:1-2).

Then Jesus appeared to him. Why then? Why didn't Jesus appear to him a few months, even a few years, earlier, before he had done all of that evil?

Because God was preparing him. To have a human instrument who would fully break with the Jewish law, who would be willing to abandon the whole thing, and instead embrace only Jesus—not Jesus and the law (see Galatians 3:1-5)—He had to show Paul the depths to which zeal for the law would take him. So when, years later,

Jewish Christians were arguing that you had to have Jesus and the law, Paul could say, in essence, "Hey, man, I've been down that law road before. I've drunk deep from that well. And let me tell you this: there's no life in the law. Life is found only in Jesus" (see Galatians 3:21).

God had to take Paul through all those experiences so he could be the man God needed. The other apostles—those who had walked with Jesus in the flesh on earth—had a harder time with these issues. Years after the Spirit came on Pentecost, Peter was still rigidly following Jewish dietary laws. God had to show him that nothing He declared clean was unclean, including believing Gentiles (see Acts 11:6-9, 15-17). Many years later, Paul *still* had to rebuke Peter publicly for acting like only Jewish believers were okay to eat with. He said to him, "Hey, the law never saved anyone, including us. We died to the law, Peter. Christ living in us, that's the whole deal" (see Galatians 2:16-21).

Paul could be the man God needed because he had traveled way down the wrong road (which, humanly speaking, seemed like the righteous road). But Jesus appeared to him personally, turned him 180 degrees, and he went away to Arabia for a while to learn directly at the feet of the ascended Christ (Galatians 1:17). He knew experientially the depths of the grace of God on someone who had erred so badly, and he knew experientially that the whole gospel was summed up in the reality of "Christ in us" (Colossians 1:27).

Am I saying someone has to go down the wrong road for years or even decades? No, that's not the point. The point is that God will take the raw material of our lives and use it to prepare us for the good works He has prepared for us to do. In my case, it did involve going down the wrong road for decades. For years I looked back on all of that and thought, "What a waste." But it wasn't a waste. It wasn't until years later that I discovered God had been using it the whole time, preparing to do through me what He wanted to do. I was exactly the vessel that He wanted to live through in a particular way, warts and all. All of His children are.

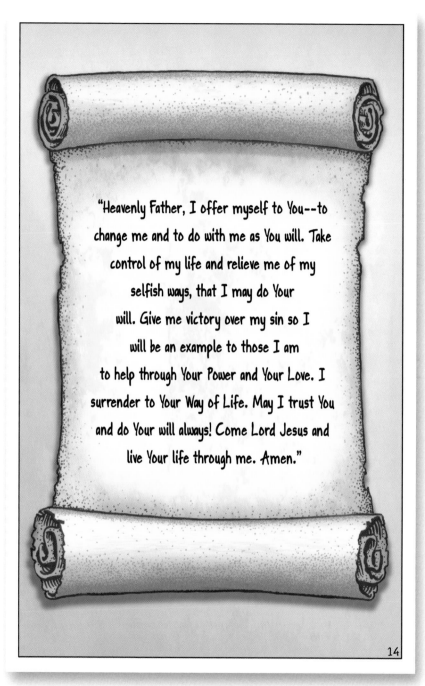

"Heavenly Father, I offer myself to You--to change me and to do with me as You will. Take control of my life and relieve me of my selfish ways, that I may do Your will. Give me victory over my sin so I will be an example to those I am to help through Your Power and Your Love. I surrender to Your Way of Life. May I trust You and do Your will always! Come Lord Jesus and live Your life through me. Amen."

14

We become vessels for God's use.

Chapter 10

My Story: God's Child

God was almost ready to bring me into His family. Of course, you could say that God had been ready all along. Certainly, He had been drawing me to Himself and putting the gospel in front of me for a long time.

But I wasn't ready. I was like a lot of people I've met over the years. I heard the gospel, I knew God was important, I knew Jesus was His Son, but somehow I never put the whole thing together.

I was getting close to the point of realizing this: *"Oh, I need to personally place my trust in Jesus! It's not enough just to have a generic belief in God. I have to make a personal choice to receive Christ by faith"* (see John 1:12).

I stumbled across an oil industry publication business that was for sale, the *Alaska Petroleum & Industrial Directory,* and I bought it. Lalla and I moved up to Anchorage. We fought all the way up the Alaska Highway with one-year-old Samantha in the back seat. At some point in the Yukon Territory, Lalla drove off without me. I got a room at a motel and somehow we found each other the next morning. It just so happened that the night before, we had separately tuned into the same Christian TV station and watched a show about reconciliation and forgiveness.

Once we got to Anchorage, we started mostly living separated at the same house. Shortly thereafter, we went to marriage counseling. They didn't have any answers. "Just get a divorce," they basically said.

One day Lalla came home from a girlfriend's house and said, "I've been with my friend, and she just got religion. She prayed over me, and I received the Spirit of God." Her friend had led her to Christ. "I'm going to join a church and take our daughter."

"Great," I replied. " When you find one you like, I'll come with you."

I had taken Lalla to a Billy Graham crusade one time in Houston. We sat up for hours talking about it. She had thought it was ridiculous, and I agreed. But now she was completely different. I watched her pick out some churches for us to visit, and read her Bible, and pray. Maybe more than anything, I watched her behavior toward me change. I started thinking, "Whatever happened to her is real and it's powerful."

So I went to a Christian bookstore to see if I could find something to help me make sense of it all. I picked up a book by Chuck Colson called *Born Again*. I respected Colson because I knew of him as a very bright guy when I worked for Nixon in Washington. He had been one of Nixon's closest counselors, and was tough as nails.

I started reading it, and I related to what he was saying. Colson said that he believed in God—he didn't see any reasonable explanation for the creation apart from a Creator—but he had never understood the Jesus thing, because guys like Colson don't mess around with sons or vice presidents. They go straight to the top. I had always thought exactly the same thing! Why mess around with God's Son instead of going straight to God?

But Colson was reading *Mere Christianity*, by C.S. Lewis, while awaiting sentencing after his Watergate trial. Lewis referred to a passage in the Gospel of John, where Jesus said, "The Father and I are one," which, John wrote, meant that Jesus was equal with God (John 5:18; 10:30-33). In other words, Jesus is God (John 1:1)! Colson said that when he understood that reality, he became a Christian. If Jesus is God, and I believed in God, I could become a follower of Jesus, too.

Suddenly the Jesus thing started clicking for me. Jesus is God!

I went to the First Baptist Church with Lalla and Samantha the next Sunday and got invited to come visit with the pastor the following Wednesday. I was in a sweat about it.

God was in the Heavens and came to earth as a man.

Philippians 2:6-8, John 1:14, Hebrews 1:3, Romans 8:3b, John 10:3
Colossians 2:9, Hebrews 2:11-17, Matthew 1:20-

1

He was conceived in a miraculous way, but He was born of a woman in the same way we were.

He did this so that we could form a personal relationship with Him and know Him as both God and man and better understand Him as Father.

My eyes were opened to who Jesus really is: *God in the flesh.*

"If we go into that preacher's office," I told her, "We're going to come out Baptists!"

When the time came, I was prepared. "You need to know that I'm an alcoholic," I exclaimed to the preacher the minute we got there.

I expected him to point a finger at me and yell, "Repent, you sinner!" Isn't that what Baptist preachers were supposed to do? Instead, he quietly told me that his sister was married to an alcoholic, but she refused to go to Al-Anon meetings or even to church.

I was a bit taken aback by his response, and so I went directly to my comfort zone and began talking AA talk.

"The key to my recovery has been acceptance," I told him, hoping to help him cope with his sister. "Acceptance of my alcoholism, acceptance of myself, acceptance of my wife. I've found that acceptance of people, places and things as creations of God is the answer. This is the only reasonable thing to do, and it's the way I'm learning to live my life."

"Fine," he replied, "are you ready to accept Jesus Christ as your personal Savior?" *I was in a trap, and I had set it for myself.*

"Of course," I said. There was nothing else to say. He led me through the sinner's prayer, but just like in Houston with my friend years before, I was mostly just there, saying the words. They hadn't become a heart reality to me yet. I needed to get out of that office and figure the whole thing out.

That night I turned on the TV and ran across Jimmy Swaggart, the evangelist (who was later involved in scandal). When Swaggart invited people to receive Christ personally by faith, I knelt in front of my TV and invited Jesus Christ to come in to my heart and take control of my life. I knew I meant it this time. Like the Apostle Paul said, I confessed with my mouth and I believed in my heart that Jesus is God and rose from the dead (Romans 10:9)! I gave my life to Him. And I knew that God meant it, too. I knew I was His.

I was 44.

I finally surrendered . . .

Day 4 — GIVE UP THE FIGHT

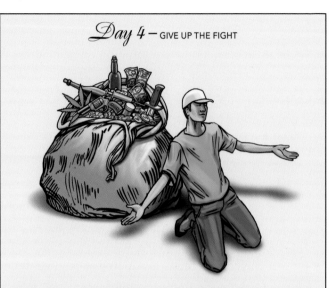

Confession, surrender, yielding and submission are all terms we must consider when we come to the end of self and make up our minds to trust Jesus as our Lord, God, Savior and Life. Acceptance of Him and His way of doing things is a form of surrender. We give up our independent way to have His life. The old gives way to the new. The old self has died and we are cleansed and made righteous with a new spiritual nature.

Because of the weakness of your human nature, I am using the illustration of slavery to help you understand all this. Previously, you let yourselves be slaves to impurity and lawlessness, which led ever deeper into sin. Now you must give yourselves to be slaves of righteous living so that you will become holy. Romans 6:19 NLT

Then Jesus said to his disciples, "If any of you wants to be my follower, you must turn from your selfish ways, take up your cross and follow me. If you try to hang on to your old life, you will lose it. But if you give up your life for my sake, you will save it." Matthew 16:24-25 NLT

63

I finally surrendered . . .

One day, someone came along and explained the story of Jesus, how He came to save each of us from eternal death by dying for us and giving us His eternal life. Jesus died, giving us all a way out, a way to experience total forgiveness, unconditional love, and hope of eternal life through Him.

Ezekiel 36:26-27, Acts 4:12, Romans 5:9, 1 Corinthians 15:57, 2 Corinthians 5:18a, Galatians1:15-16, Ephesians 2:8-9, 1 Timothy 2:5-6

8

. . . and received God's gift.

. . . and received God's gift.

Looking back at all the years before this, I see that God simply wants us to surrender to Him, to give up the fight, to receive what He has already freely given in His Son. We all have to reach that point. If I had done that many years before—if I had gone to a more evangelical church in my youth where the gospel was clearly presented and I had been challenged to turn my life over to Christ—I could have avoided decades of destruction and waste.

But God had a different path for me. I had to accept that He knew what it took to get me to this point, and that He would even use all those "wasted" years to His glory. I had no idea the degree to which He would do that.

I knew one thing: I was going to go at this Jesus thing exactly the same way I had gone at whiskey—all or nothing. I felt determined to find out everything I could about this new experience.

Chapter 11

What Actually Happened

The truth is that I really didn't know what all had happened to me the night I put my faith in Jesus. Almost no believers do. It was Watchman Nee who said (this is a paraphrase) that if we could teach people the full extent of everything God did to them and for them the moment they came to Christ, we'd save them a lot of grief finding out the hard way through years of trying and failing to live the Christian life.

Unfortunately, very few of us are taught that way. I didn't have anyone to tell me those things immediately either, but God had His own plan to teach me.

Years later, through some excellent training materials and my own study of Scripture, I came to understand much more clearly what happened to me that night—what happens to all of us who have joined ourselves to Christ. It's easy to stop short of everything Christ accomplished through the cross. Oh, we all sort of get the forgiveness of sins part, of course. And we all get the idea that somehow the Holy Spirit comes to us, and that He will somehow guide us and help us.

But a whole lot more happened to us when we placed our trust in Christ—when we received the new birth—than that. When we were born from above, God performed a heart transplant on us. Through Ezekiel, He told the Jews that that's exactly what He would do one day, under a new covenant. He explained:

> I will give you a new heart and put a new spirit within you; and
> I will remove the heart of stone from your flesh and give you a
> heart of flesh. (Ezekiel 36:26)

God isn't talking about giving them the Holy Spirit here. That comes in the next verse. In this verse, God says that He will actually give them a new heart. He will take the old heart out and give them a new heart. *Then*, He says,

> I will put My Spirit within you. (Ezekiel 36:27a)

This is exactly what Jesus explained to Nicodemus in John 3. "You must be born again," Jesus said to him. And He explained what that meant:

> Unless one is born of water and the Spirit he cannot enter into the kingdom of God. That which is born of the flesh is flesh, and that which is born of the Spirit is spirit. (John 3:5)

What is Jesus saying here? Exactly what Ezekiel was saying: that the Holy Spirit literally gives birth to a new spirit (a new heart) within us. God doesn't just forgive us and leave us the way we were, with a sinful heart in rebellion against Him. He takes that heart out and gives us a new one. He brings into being someone who didn't exist before. We become, as Paul said, new creations in Christ:

> Therefore if anyone is in Christ, he is a new creature; the old things passed away; behold, new things have come. (2 Corinthians 5:17)

Now, Paul says, "all things are from God" (2 Corinthians 5:18). Everything about who we truly are now is from God. This is the new man in Christ, "created in holiness and righteousness of the truth" (Ephesians 4:24). Through the new birth we are created holy and righteous. We aren't simply *declared* righteous (although God does do that as well). We actually *are* righteous—the righteousness of God in Christ (2 Corinthians 5:21). That's why John writes:

> Little children, make sure no one deceives you; the one who practices righteousness is righteous, just as He is righteous. (1 John 3:7)

How could we expect anything less than God actually making us righteous in our inner being? If the Holy Spirit gives birth to a new spirit within us, what would we expect that new spirit, that new heart, to be? Sinful? That's preposterous. He is going to birth within us a new spirit with the exact same nature as Him. That's why Paul says our new man is "created in holiness and righteousness."

Someone will say, "Yeah, but I still sin. So my old man is still there. I'm either still a sinner at heart, or at best I'm part old man, part new man."

It's understandable why people think that. We somehow have to make sense of the fact that, as believers in Christ, we still sin. So, we assess truth based on our experience. But experience is a poor source for ultimate truth. What God actually says is truth.

Here's what God says happened to our old man:

> ... *knowing this, that our old man was crucified with Him* ... (Romans 6:6)

Our old man died. He didn't just get moved over a bit to make room for the new man. He died. God killed him off. How did this happen? When we received Christ, we were made one spirit with Him.

> *He who joins himself to the Lord is one spirit with Him.* (1 Corinthians 6:17)

We are one with Christ, which is exactly what Jesus asked the Father to do (John 17:21). Because of that, what happened to Him, happened to us:

- *We died with Him*
  (Romans 7:4; Galatians 2:19-20; 2 Corinthians 5:14; Colossians 3:3)

- *We were buried with Him*
  (Romans 6:4; Colossians 2:12)

- *We were raised with Him*
  (Ephesians 2:6; Colossians 2:12-13; 3:1)

- *We are now seated with Christ in the heavenly realm*
  (Ephesians 2:6)

- *Jesus Himself came to live in us*
  (John 14:20; Galatians 2:20; Colossians 1:27)

We were crucified with Him, buried with Him, raised with Him, and now we are seated with Him in the very presence of God.

For He raised us up from the dead along with Christ and seated us with Him in the Heavenly realms because we are united with Christ Jesus.

Ephesians 2:6, NLT

29

We are already seated with Christ in the heavenlies.

Paul doesn't talk about all of this in figurative language, *as if* we had died with Christ. He says over and over that we *did* die with Christ. Our old self ceased to exist. We are the new man in Christ.

How did God accomplish this? Jesus died on the cross 2,000 years ago. How can God say we died with Him? There are spiritual realities here that, admittedly, are difficult to fully grasp. But God says that they are true. I find that it helps to realize that God exists completely outside of time. If He says He put our old man on the cross with Christ (which is the spiritual part of us, not the physical), who am I to argue?

When you ask Jesus Christ to come into your life, you are transferred out of the lineage of your earthly family in Adam and into the eternal life of Christ, **the life that is forever in the past and forever in the future.** You are transferred to the cross and the old self dies with Christ.

Romans 5:18-19, Romans 8:1-2, 1 Corinthians 15:22, Galatians 5:24, Ephesians 1:13-14, Ephesians 3:14-15, 1 Peter 1:18-19

17

We become one with Christ. Our old self literally died with Him.

You become one with Him. You are united with Christ, and that will never change. Jesus now lives in you and you in Him. Wherever He goes, you go. Wherever you go, He goes.

John 14:20, Romans 6:6, Galatians 2:20, Galatians 4:4-7, Galatians 5:24, Ephesians 1:11, Colossians 2:10

18

It is vital to realize that, from our time-based perspective, this happens to us the moment we place our faith in Christ. Paul never talks about our death, burial, and resurrection with Christ as a process, or something we are *trying* to do. It is not something that we do at all. It is entirely something that God does for us, and in us. It is already a done deal for all who have put their faith in Christ and joined themselves to Him (1 Corinthians 6:17). God simply tells us to count on it (Romans 6:11-13).

But someone will say, "Yes, but I still sin! Why, if I am a new man?" Paul explains why. We still live in unredeemed bodies, and the power of sin still *operating in the members of our unredeemed physical bodies* can drag us down (Romans 7:23). But, as much as it may feel like it, there is not a civil war going on in our inner man. Our inner man is completely on God's side (Romans 7:22). We are new creations in Christ. The old things are gone. Now all things are from God. God birthed within us a righteous, holy new man (Ephesians 4:24).

How vital this truth is became most apparent to me when I started corresponding with prisoners. These are men (and women) who often have done what we consider as bad things. They don't need a gospel that just says, "God forgives you, and He'll help you try to be a better person." It's wonderful news that God forgives us, but trying to be a better person, and God helping us out a little doesn't cut it for these folks. They know that they need something radically different now, not by when we die a physical death. They realize they need a complete spiritual makeover. Somehow, someway they need to know they really are brand new people. Literally, born again! How to be a child of God tells this story clearly and completely.

The good news is that Jesus provides complete forgiveness and a complete spiritual makeover. Many Christ followers don't fully realize how totally Jesus did away with the sin issue between us and God. The writer to the Hebrews said that Jesus appeared the first time to put away sin (Hebrews 9:26). The word means to annul, set aside, or cancel. The Greek word literally means "no longer having a place." Because of what Jesus did at the cross, sin no longer has a place in our relationship with God. Jesus completely took care of it. All of our sins have been forgiven (Colossians 2:13), past, present, and future. God does not take them into account (Romans 4:7-8). There is never, ever any condemnation for us who are in Christ (Romans 8:1).

People who have led lives that put them in prison desperately need to know that they are completely forgiven. I should know—a good number of the cards and letters I receive say, "Tell me more about God's forgiveness." The wonderful news is that God has wiped the slate clean, and in Christ it stays clean!

They also need to know that God remakes them completely on the inside. He makes them completely new creations. Then He

Himself comes to live in them. The Life invades their hearts. Their own lives truly can be radically different from this day forward because Jesus makes them different. The old—including all they may have done—has passed away. New things have come! Now all things are from God.

Through Christ's full work at the cross, God has given us everything pertaining to life and godliness (2 Peter 1:3). He doesn't save us and say, "Okay, do the best you can. Good luck!" The true good news of Jesus goes way, way beyond that, as God was about to show me.

When your "old self" died with Jesus on the Cross, you also were buried with Him. Your new spiritual self comes to life with Christ and ascends into the Heavenly places with Him. You left behind the bag of shortcomings, guilt, sins and shame. You are in Christ, and He is in you. You exchange your old life for a new one. You now have the Spirit of God in you and your human spirit has been restored to life with God. You are in Christ and along for the great ride of your eternal life. YOU ARE REBORN!

John 3:6, John 11:25-26, Romans 5:5, Romans 6:4-6, Romans 8:10, Colossians 2:12-14, Colossians 3:1-3, Ephesians 1:13b, Ephesians 2:6

19

A completely new creation.

# Chapter 12

My Story: God Reveals the Whole Thing

After we both put our faith in Christ, my wife Lalla and I started taking a discipleship course with the pastor of First Baptist Anchorage, going through a book by Ralph Neighbor called *Survival Kit for New Christians*. (I later worked with Ralph in his ministry in Houston.) What I kept hearing and reading was that walking with Christ was all about faith. If I really wanted all Christ had to offer, I had to increase my faith. But how?

Then I came across a verse, Romans 10:17: "Faith comes from hearing and hearing by the Word of God." So, I bought a cassette tape of the Book of Romans and I proceeded to listen to it day and night. I must have listened to it 200 to 300 times. And it worked! My faith increased dramatically.

From early on in my new life, God was teaching me that His Word could powerfully change people. I needed to know that deeply when, decades later, God chose me as the vessel He would use to transform the lives of many in prison.

God still had a lot to change in me as well. Lalla and I were hardly fully transformed into our new life, and we continued to fight. It got pretty bad and finally I left and went back to Houston. I had threatened to do so many times. At least in Houston I had a friend to stay with and keep studying the Bible, learning to live out this new creation that I had become. I wanted to find out what happened to me and what it really meant that I had been "saved."

The following Sunday I went to Second Baptist Church in Houston.

One of their pastors, Jim DeLoach, was preaching. After the service, I approached him and told him I was a new Christian.

"I need a sponsor in Christianity," I told him, and wanted to see if he was available. I was still talking the AA talk!

He cocked his head in a funny sort of way and said, "I don't quite understand what you're asking, but I can tell you I would be proud to serve in that capacity."

I told Jim that as my sponsor he would need to be careful what he told me, as I was going to do whatever he said.

He said, "Great. Come to the chapel next Sunday at 8:30 and sit in on a Bible study that Jane Elder and I teach."

"I can't come at 8:30. I have an AA meeting that hour."

He replied, "I said, 'Come at 8:30 to the building next door.'"

I had just finished saying I'd do whatever he told me. "I'll be there."

Jim DeLoach was my friend and discipler (my sponsor in Christianity!) for the next 35 years, until he passed away not long ago. Jane Elder, his co-teacher, would help guide my life as well. In fact, throughout my Christian life and until they died, I rarely did anything of consequence around the church without checking with one of them first.

The following month was mission's month at Second Baptist. Jane Elder was mission's director at the church. She told me that the church wanted to give some money to start churches in Alaska, and she asked me to give my testimony at a Wednesday night service about coming to Christ up there. I was happy to do so. I had done that kind of thing all the time at AA.

A week later Jane informed me that the church had just voted to give $50,000 to my church in Anchorage. Two days later I called my pastor in Anchorage to talk about my family.

"By the way," I said, "Second Baptist in Houston has voted to send you $50,000."

I figured churches must do this kind of thing all the time. I didn't know any better. My pastor, however, was floored. He said that two nights before, on Wednesday night, the church leaders had asked God to provide $50,000 to buy the property they wanted for a new mission church plant.

This was my first exposure to the wonderful, miraculous power of God answering prayer and taking care of His children. Incidents like this seemed to happen regularly to me, strengthening my faith. Jim DeLoach had taught me to watch for and acknowledge answered prayers. Knowing God answers prayer greatly strengthened my faith.

About that time, a friend suggested I go see a Christian counselor in Boerne, Texas, near San Antonio. I went over there for a week. I learned some wonderful principles there about how unresolved parent issues of both partners can impact a marriage. Essentially, I was learning with each lesson that I was to rely totally on Christ. A lifetime of old habits of relating must be broken. These are hard lessons to learn.

I called Lalla and asked her to come down for a week for joint counseling. She flew to Houston, and we spent the afternoon at the DeLoach's house. That afternoon Jim said something I've never forgotten.

"Remember," he said, "whenever one of you speaks to the other, it is God talking to you through that person. He lives in us."

Lalla almost gagged when she heard Jim say that. And, on my part, I became a much better listener to her. Usually.

I have used that wise counsel with many couples over the years. I'm certain it makes better listeners of them all. If they can listen better, then they can hear God urging them to love and forgive.

Lalla and I went back to Alaska together to start over. We were both on fire for Jesus and we sought out opportunities to learn and be discipled anywhere we could find them. Somehow God gave us discernment as to what was good teaching and what was not. We had both initially been taught that the Bible was the inerrant Word of God, and that helped guide us tremendously. If a teacher didn't line up with God's Word, we didn't go back for more.

One night I reverted to my old ways and started an argument with Lalla. I'd found out she went out with a guy while I was gone and I was upset about it, since we were still married. We fought verbally all night, bickering and making accusations, and things kept escalating. Finally, she picked up the phone and called Jim DeLoach. I had told her Jim was my "sponsor," of course, and the Holy Spirit nudged her to call him.

When she hung up, I asked her, "What did Jim say?"

"He said for you to get on your knees and ask forgiveness."

I got on my knees in front of her and began to ask God for forgiveness. Instantly, I saw a light in the distance which came closer and closer. As it appeared within a few feet of me, the light became an image of Jesus. He was nailed to a tree. Blood was pouring from pores all over His body, as if He were sweating blood, and He was writhing in agony. I continued to pray and ask for forgiveness, and I noticed that my body was swaying in agony, in concert with His. The agony was not physical, but emotional. I saw and felt the emotional pain of Jesus as a result of my sin. It was all as clear to me, as real to me, as Lalla sitting there in the room with me.

At that moment, God showed me the whole package. I was one with Christ. What He experienced, I experienced. What happened to Him, happened to me. When He died, I died.

I called Jim back and told him about my encounter.

He simply said, "Galatians 2:20. 'I have been crucified with Christ, and it is no longer I who live, but Christ lives in me, and the life which I now live in the flesh I live by faith in the Son of God, who loved me, and delivered Himself up for me.'"

That verse, as it turns out, has been the foundation of everything I believe about how the Christian life is to be lived.

I have been crucified with Christ. The old David Howell died. He's not around anymore. God joined him to Christ on the cross and crucified Him. What he was a part of, seeking life in earthly things, I'm not a part of anymore.

It is no longer I who live. The former "I" has ceased to exist. A new "me" has been born and has been raised up with Christ. I am a new creation (2 Corinthians 5:17). As Paul said, since I have been raised up with Christ, and since my life is hidden with Christ in God, I seek the things above (Colossians 3:3-4). But it is not even the new "me" that is really living this life now.

But Christ lives in me. The one who is actually living this life within me now is Christ. He loves through me, forgives through me, speaks through me, acts through me. I am a vessel He has chosen to live through.

And the life which I now live in the flesh . . . I am alive. I do live in this physical body.

I live by faith in the Son of God. I'm not living by my effort to

My old self has been crucified with Christ. It is no longer I who live, but Christ lives in me. So I live in this earthly body by trusting in the Son of God, who loved me and gave Himself for me.

Galatians 2:20, NLT

30

It is no longer I who live, but Christ lives in me.

pull off the Christian life. I'm not trying to live this life at all. I'm trusting that Christ within me is completely adequate in every situation, and that He is living through me.

Who loved me and delivered Himself up for me? The incredible reality of God's love is forever shown at the cross, where the Son of God Himself died for me, because He loved me, a lost son, and wanted to bring me back to Him.

In a real sense, God simply took me on a shortcut and showed me the totality of the gospel right after I came to Christ. He showed me my union with Christ. The gospel isn't just that Christ died for us so our sins could be forgiven. That's half the gospel. The other half is that we died with Him, that we were raised with Him as new creations, and that He Himself comes to live in us, living His very life through us. When Paul wrote to the Colossians, he explained to them that the primary message God had given him to preach was this: Christ in you (Colossians 1:24-27). Christ in us is the very center of the gospel. God Himself comes to live in humans! Doesn't it make sense that that would be life-changing?

Why did God show me my union with Christ right off the bat? So many Christians wait decades figuring that out if they ever do at all. I was certainly no more worthy of it than any other believer. Less, from a human standpoint!

All I can figure is that God knew that I would need the complete message to share with prisoners one day, because half of the message wasn't going to cut it with people as desperate as they are. I was already 44, and I would need to learn how to effectively share the message of the whole gospel, and I didn't have decades to wander around, trying to figure out the truth. I had to know it now!

But within the first few months after I came to Christ, I was already getting frustrated, going through the Bible, trying to wade through and categorize and implement all of these hundreds of rules for behavior (if we interpret them as rules) in the New Testament, which are just as numerous (and harder to keep!) as the ones in the Old. I was dead serious about following Jesus as best I could, and I thought the way to do that was to turn the whole thing into another Law-based system.

I think it's almost as if the Father turned to the Son one day and said,

"This guy's never going to be ready for the work we've prepared for him to do unless we put him on the right track. He's going to need a simple way to share the whole gospel down the road."

So that's what God did. I could have spent decades having my understanding muddled with inadequate doctrine, hopelessly bogged down, trying to figure out the Christian life. Instead, Jesus just said, "Here it is. You're one with me. When I died, you died. When I was buried and raised, you were buried and raised. When I was seated at the right hand of the Father, you were seated. It's already done. Now I live in you. Just be a willing vessel, and I will do my works through you."

That's the message that desperate people need (and so do people who don't even know they are desperate, but really are). The gospel is not, "Get forgiven by Jesus and then try really hard to be a good Christian." That treadmill doesn't work! It just wears people out. But Jesus said, "My yoke is easy and my burden is light" (Matthew 11:30).

Was Jesus joking? How can living this out possibly be easy and light? Because we are not really the ones living it! Christ is the only one who can live out His own life. As Paul said, "It is no longer I who live, but Christ lives in me" (Galatians 2:20). The gospel is Christ in us.

Men sitting in solitary confinement, at the end of their self-reliance, need a message that brings true life. They need a miracle. God is offering them a miracle. They need to know that Christ wants to come inside and be their very life. Now!

Jesus wants to live through men and women in prison. He has thousands of people He wants to reach in there through them, and those men and women become His arms and legs, part of His own body, carrying the message. He wants to live through each of us in our own unique way to reach the world. For a prisoner, it may simply be another prisoner saying, "Hey, what happened to you?" and him replying, "Here, read this booklet." It doesn't have to be any more complicated than that. Jesus lives in us and reaches the world through us, just as we are. That's exactly how He has made us to be, so He could do through us the work He planned to do. If He can do that through men and women in jails and prisons—if He could do that through me—He can do it through anyone.

Since I live, you also will live. When I am raised to life again, you will know that I am in My Father, and you are in Me, and I am in you.
John 14:19b-20, NLT

"You are in Me, and I am in you."

Chapter 13

Helping New Believers Grow

Once I started sending *How to Be a Child of God* into prisons and I started hearing from inmates, one thing became obvious: the inmates were hungry for follow-up. They had entered into a new relationship with God (or maybe some already knew Jesus, but had badly neglected that relationship), and they wanted to know how to grow in that relationship.

How to Be a Child of God, of course, already laid the foundation for Christian growth. I think that's why it was getting read over and over.

It's easy to get our attention diverted from that which is central. We focus on the spiritual things or service work that we are supposed to do, much of which can be very helpful. But that's not the center of the Christian life. Jesus is. Our lives are now lived moment by moment by faith in Him.

This is the heart of the Christian life—living by faith in Christ in us. The entire Christian life is a walk of faith. "The righteous shall live by faith" the New Testament says three times (Romans 1:17; Galatians 3:11; Hebrews 10:38). "We walk by faith, not by sight," Paul told the Corinthians (2 Corinthians 5:7). "As you have received Christ Jesus the Lord, so walk in Him," Paul wrote to the Colossians (2:6). How did we receive Him? *By faith.*

How to Be a Child of God already laid out this reality. I could tell from their letters that, as inmates read it repeatedly, that message began to sink in. *"Oh, I get it! I died with Christ. The old me is gone. I was raised a new me. Christ lives in me now. He is here to*

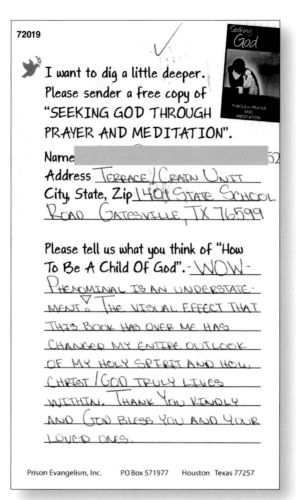

72019

I want to dig a little deeper.
Please sender a free copy of
"SEEKING GOD THROUGH
PRAYER AND MEDITATION".

Seeking
God

THROUGH PRAYER
AND
MEDITATION

Name ▮▮▮▮▮▮▮▮▮▮ 52

Address TERRACE / CRAIN UNIT

City, State, Zip 1401 STATE SCHOOL
ROAD GATESVILLE, TX 76599

Please tell us what you think of "How
To Be A Child Of God". - WOW -
PHENOMINAL IS AN UNDERSTATE-
MENT. THE VISUAL EFFECT THAT
THIS BOOK HAS OVER ME HAS
CHANGED MY ENTIRE OUTLOOK
OF MY HOLY SPIRIT AND HOW
CHRIST / GOD TRULY LIVES
WITHIN. THANK YOU KINDLY
AND GOD BLESS YOU AND YOUR
LOVED ONES.

Prison Evangelism, Inc.   PO Box 571977   Houston Texas 77257

live His life through me. He does that as I trust Him to do it."

I would get letters that said things like, "I read your book five times. Then I posted the prayer in the book on my wall. I say it every night. I know that Christ lives in me!"

All of the spiritual things that we can do are really just meant to point us more in this direction, of living by faith in Christ in us.

I wanted to put something together to help them do that. Specifically, I wanted to teach them how to spend time with God in prayer and Scripture-based meditation. I remembered as a young Christian (young in my 40s!) being told to pray and meditate on Scripture, and I thought, "Great. How do I do that?"

So I put together a follow-up booklet, called *Seeking God Through*

Seeking God

THROUGH PRAYER AND MEDITATION
Devotional Edition

Helping believers grow in their relationship with God.

Prayer and Meditation. It not only instructs people how to pray and do Scripture-based meditation, but also has a 30-day devotional to help them constantly be reminded of how to grow in their understanding of Christ as their life.

I also wanted a resource that specifically helped inmates understand the incredible change that God had made inside them when they placed their faith in Him. I wanted them to know

Fully Alive *and* Finally Free

Knowing God
As Father

David Howell

Helping believers understand the incredible change God made inside them, and the reality of Christ living in them.

that they had been made entirely new, that God had given them a new heart, and that Jesus Himself had come to live in them, to live His life through them. So I put together one more booklet, *Fully Alive and Finally Free*.

I also put a perforated card at the end of *How to Be a Child of God*, a postcard, that had my address on one side and said on the other side:

I want to dig a little deeper. Please send me a free copy of *Seeking God Through Prayer and Meditation.*

It has a place for their name and address, and anything they might want to comment about the first booklet.

I get twenty to thirty of those cards a day. That's over 7,000 inmates a year who have not only read *How to Be a Child of God*, but want follow-up material and take the time to fill out the card and pay to put a stamp on it and send it to me. And I'm just amazed. I realize that these cards that I get back are just the tip of the iceberg. Many times, that number are reading the booklets and God is at work in their lives. The cards and letters on the following three pages are typical.

These cards are like personal devotionals for me. I read them and see how God is moving in these men and women's lives and I praise Him.

I do what they ask me to do, of course. I put *Seeking God Through Prayer and Meditation* in mailers, put their prison addresses on them, take them to the post office, and mail them. On a typical day, it takes me about three hours. Often I get letters in return. A lot of them say things like,

"I've been a Christian a long time, but your book helped me understand in a way I never did before. I know now that Jesus lives in me. I want Him to live His life through me."

When they write something like that, I know they get it. They understand the message God sent Paul to preach: Christ in you.

72019

🕊 I want to dig a little deeper. Please sender a free copy of "SEEKING GOD THROUGH PRAYER AND MEDITATION".

Name ▬▬▬▬▬▬▬▬
Address 150 W. HEDDING St.
City, State, Zip San Jose,
    California 95110

Please tell us what you think of "How To Be A Child Of God". I Gave My life to GOD And accept Jesus CHrist as my LorD and Savior. This Book changed my Life my Thinking.

GOD   Thank
Bless   you.

Prison Evangelism, Inc.   PO Box 571977   Houston Texas 77257

72019

🕊 I want to dig a little deeper. Please sender a free copy of "SEEKING GOD THROUGH PRAYER AND MEDITATION".

Name ▬▬▬▬▬▬▬▬
Address   P.O. BOX 1382
City, State, Zip Sinton TX 78387

Please tell us what you think of "How To Be A Child Of God". This is the best thing I have ever came into contact with. It has completely changed my life and this is the book I share with everyone who wants to hear it.

72019

🕊 I want to dig a little deeper. Please sender a free copy of "SEEKING GOD THROUGH PRAYER AND MEDITATION".

Name ▬▬▬▬▬▬▬ 31
Address EWCC D-4   PO Box 315
City, State, Zip Taft, OK
    74463-0315

Please tell us what you think of "How To Be A Child Of God". This book has changed my life! It explained things to me in a way I could understand. W/ this deeper understanding came greater meaning. I am now enrolled in Bible College. I have sent a copy of this book to my 11 yr. old daughter. I now talk about Jesus Christ w/ my family. Life is getting real good because of God.

Prison Evangelism, Inc.   PO Box 571977   Houston Texas 77257

720

🕊 I want to dig a little deeper. Please sender a free copy of "SEEKING GOD THROUGH PRAYER AND MEDITATION".

Name ▬▬▬▬▬▬▬
Address 200 West Court Street
City, State, Zip Yuma, ARIZONA
85364

Please tell us what you think of "How To Be A Child Of God". That book was exactly what I was looking for and needed because I honestly did not know how to be a child of God.

Prison Evangelism, Inc.   PO Box 571977   Houston Texas 77257

Breaking Into Prison   83

Jamestown, CA - 93327

20 Jan. 2020

Dear David,

Peace & blessings be upon you. Thank you for sending me "Seeking God Through prayer & Meditation". I thuroughly enjoyed it. You'll be happy to know I've passed it along & in fact so many people expressed interest in it there's a chain 7 long waiting for it to be passed along to each in turn. I'm sure there will be more too.

I want you to know your message was clear & the art really helped visualize Jesus living within us & what He experiences with us. That we become living temples of God when we are saved by faith. The design makes it easier to share with folks who may be put off or intimidated by lengthy intellectual seeking texts. It's inviting & easy to follow. It lays out a good plan for creating a more robust prayer life & the 31 day devotional at the end was helpful.

Just wanted to share that with you. I was baptized 8 days ago & am appreciative of the time & effort y'all put into getting the gospel into places like this & the tools for us to share what we learn with others. Thank you.

Take care & God continue to keep & bless you.

Respectfully

I have not read Seeking God through prayer and meditation but my cellmate has been reading it for the last two days. Since he has begun reading this book I have noticed a drastic change in his behavior and outlook on life. He has become very humble and seems to be at peace. I have the book next to read but seen the influence it has over my cellmate and would like to ask for my own copy of "Seeking God through prayer and meditation. I'm currently housed at (NDOC) Nevada Department of Correction. High Desert State prison. I know God knows me and is constantly looking out for me but I want to give myself to him completely. I am a sinner and wish to ask forgivness. Please help me become a child of God so I can save my soul and spread his word to other misguided souls, please & Thank you.

new believer

Chapter 14

My Story: God's Evangelism Training

After my encounter with Jesus, I kind of figured that was the norm for Christians. After all, believers in the New Testament (to say nothing of the Old) had visions, didn't they? I discovered otherwise. Several times shortly after my encounter, I shared it with other believers at Bible studies and home groups that we went to—even with pastors. People looked at me like I was absolutely crazy. One pastor said, "Oh, so you saw God?" I got that message four or five times, and I learned to keep my mouth shut until more opportune times arose. Which is a shame, really.

Nevertheless, Lalla and I got very active in ministry. We bought movies like *Jesus of Nazareth* and invited friends, both Christians and non-Christians, over to watch and discuss. Soon we had the first pew in our church filled with people we had known in AA and Al-Anon. All had been blind, but now they could see. God had gifted me to witness and was training me to be an evangelist.

Lalla and I found out that a Billy Graham crusade was coming to Anchorage. I wanted to be involved. Lalla and I had been crashing every training and discipleship conference—even pastors conferences—in Alaska, just trying to learn more and more. We were never on an invitation list. We just showed up and signed up on the spot. No one ever turned us away.

Billy Graham put out a call for every church to send its ten best people to a six-week intensive counselor training course to prepare for the crusade. These people would be the ones who would share Christ with those who came down when Billy Graham gave the invitation to receive Christ.

We figured we wouldn't qualify for this course, either, so we just showed up and signed in. Three thousand people attended the training. These were pastors, assistant pastors, deacons—church leaders, mostly. During the six weeks, 350 of them came to know Jesus. That many had shown up, not even knowing Jesus, but came to know Him while taking an evangelism course!

I learned a great lesson. Never assume a person is saved. Confront them. Ask them the right questions and find out. Present the gospel of Jesus Christ. Watch God work.

At the end of the six weeks, Lalla and I filled out applications as volunteers. We figured they would have us help direct cars in the stadium parking lot, or do child care, or whatever. But they asked who wanted to be in a leadership position at the crusade, and Lalla and I raised our hands. (We had been Christians less than a year at this point.) Over the next few weeks they kept cutting the group down in size, and some people dropped out, and finally the group was down to 22 people, and the crusade director said, "You 22 are going to lead this crusade."

And I thought, "How in the world did I get here? I could be a Mormon, for all they know. And they certainly don't know I've only been a Christian for less than a year!"

Then the director asked all of us to give our testimony of coming to Christ, and I thought, "Bingo. Here's where the proof lies. It's kind of hard to make up a testimony of coming to know Christ if you don't know Him."

So Lalla and I were on the leadership team, and we also counseled people who came forward each night at the invitation. The young Inuit girls seemed particularly attracted to Lalla, and sometimes two or three would be waiting to be counseled by her before she could even leave the stands to come down to the podium where Dr. Graham would speak to them.

God's hand was totally in all of this. Neither Lalla nor I were capable of this, and we knew it. What a faith builder! Even though we were young in the faith, we had all the rights and privileges that being children of God afforded and bestowed. Christ was living through us.

After a few more months, we moved back to Houston. We joined

Second Baptist Church and Ralph Neighbor's Through the Bible in One Year class there. Ralph taught heavily on Galatians 2:20:

> I have been crucified with Christ, and it is no longer I who live but Christ lives in me...

God had already shown me the reality of that verse personally, and it was central to my whole view of the Christian life (and, clearly, it was for the Apostle Paul, too!).

I became director of the class, which soon overflowed the fellowship hall and had to move to a larger spot. We were also heavily involved with Ralph's cell group ministry. Later, Ralph left the church to run his own ministry and Lalla and I both went to work for him at Touch Ministries. I was doing his marketing via direct mail and his product development, including small group courses, leadership manuals, and cassette tapes. God was taking all of my training and experience in publishing and was now teaching me to use it in ministry.

We continued to be heavily involved at Second Baptist, manning phone prayer lines, helping to lead the prayer ministry, building databases, teaching discipleship classes and prayer classes, taking counselor training and doing one-on-one counseling. My primary mentor was Jim DeLoach, the associate pastor, followed by Jane Elder, the mission's director, who both became dear friends.

In 1991, our Senior Pastor, Dr. Ed Young, was being installed as president of the Southern Baptist Convention (SBC) in Indianapolis. I asked four men (all part of the prayer ministry I was involved in) if they'd like to drive up there with me for the nationwide conference. They agreed.

I asked Jim DeLoach if he could find some work for us to do at the convention. He said, "How wonderful that you guys want to go to the convention so you can pray for your pastor." I wasn't even thinking about that, but that became our job! We piled into a van and took off for Indianapolis, praying as we went.

On the way up and back we listened to some teaching tapes that one of the guys had brought along. As it turned out, the whole tape series focused on Galatians 2:20, what God did to us at the new birth, and the reality of Christ living in us, and through us. I loved it! When we got back to Houston, I sought out the ministry that had produced the tapes and ended up going through an extensive, year-long discipleship training with them, all of which expanded upon what God had already showed me that night in the vision He gave me.

When we finally got to the convention hall in Indianapolis, we walked to the front and met Dr. Charles Stanley, the famous preacher and outgoing president of the SBC. He said, "We heard you were coming. Station your people around the podium, wherever you need to be. Just do what you need to do to pray for your pastor." So, we basically had the run of the whole convention, which was wonderful. I love being in that atmosphere, with thousands of men called by God to serve. It always thrills me.

When we got back from Indianapolis, I took the 12 hours of material we had listened to about Christ in us, and our identity in Christ, and boiled the whole thing down to a one-hour presentation. Mainly, I wanted to do it to get it down pat and make it a permanent part of my thinking. They say that the best way to learn material is to teach it. Later I gave a condensed presentation to most of the leadership of Second Baptist as well as a bunch of other folks, about 100 in total. God was giving me a message bigger than just "Jesus died for the forgiveness of your sins." This was great practice in sharing a more complete gospel message with people.

During this time Second Baptist wanted to ordain me as a deacon. I didn't think I was qualified because of my two prior divorces, but the staff said those divorces were before I even came to Christ, so they ordained me. I considered it a great honor and privilege. I had experienced forgiveness from God, and to experience forgiveness from man was simply a validation of the fullness of God's grace.

Sometime later, I was asked to teach a Sunday morning adult class of young singles (many of whom were divorced). I declined, however. Being one of the Sunday teachers was a high calling, and I didn't feel adequate for the task, either in my Bible knowledge yet or in myself as a role model. Despite both Lalla and I having become Christians and seeking to walk with God and serving in ministry, I knew that our marriage wasn't on the most solid ground, and I certainly didn't want these young people looking to emulate me.

Around that time, I went to see a Christian movie showing in the Second Baptist auditorium. In the story, space travelers (maybe angels, I don't know) were looking down from their space ship at a young man below on earth living through various life situations and one of them asked, "I wonder if there will be a proclaimer for him when he is ready?"

I realized that, in the vast majority of cases, there must be a proclaimer to proclaim the gospel and reveal Jesus Christ. Someone has to testify, to show a witnessing tract, or one way or another explain the good news of Jesus Christ so that a person has the opportunity to accept Him as the Lord, God, and Savior of mankind. A message or messenger can come in many forms.

At that profound moment in my life, I realized that my gift was evangelism. God had called me to witness whenever I had the opportunity, and to spread the gospel.

That was something I was already doing, of course, on my own time and also at Second Baptist. I was part of the team that met with people one on one when they would come down to the front of the church at the end of services. Sometimes they wanted to receive Christ, and I led them through that. Sometimes they just wanted to join the church, and we would start that process. Sometimes they had been members of another church and wanted to switch membership to Second. Experience taught me to ask the right questions to make sure they had actually received Christ. Many times, I found they hadn't! They had been sitting in pews for years but had never understood that they needed to personally put their faith in Jesus and receive Him into their lives.

In particular, I usually asked the question that God had confronted me with through the book *Born Again*, by Chuck Colson: "Do you believe that Jesus is God?"

A lot of people—even church people—responded, "Well, I believe he's the Son of God."

The minute they said that I knew where we needed to start. "In the beginning was the Word," John wrote. "And the Word was with God. And the Word was God" (John 1:1-2).

Over time, I probably met with 3,000 people in this way. God used these 3,000 one-on-one encounters to hone my thinking as to the most effective way to communicate the gospel to people. He was at work, equipping me, step by step, for the work He had prepared me to do.

Chapter 15

My Story: More Very Raw Material

In 1990, Second Baptist asked both Lalla and me to come on staff with the church. They wanted Lalla to work in the music department and I was to be in the pastoral department.

This wasn't the first time I was offered or I sought a position in full time vocational ministry. Looking back, I believe God was strongly guiding my path, keeping me on the road toward the work He had prepared for me. That's His job, keeping us on the path, even if we take a few detours. He uses it all as His raw material. But we have to be willing. If I had taken one or more of those jobs, who knows how sidetracked I might have become, wrapped up in a different kind of ministry. God had other plans.

In this case, however, when Second Baptist offered both Lalla and me positions, I think it was different. I believe God really was calling us to that. But, I reasoned myself out of it. At that point in life, we had two young girls, Samantha and Clementine. I felt we just couldn't make it work financially on what we would be paid, so I declined. Subconsciously, I think I also knew that my marriage was still not in good shape. But I think the real truth was that I was simply being disobedient. I believe that had I answered God's call and done what He told me to do, I would have seen a special blessing on me, our marriage, and our family. All of our lives would have taken a dramatic positive turn. As it happened, my life would become very complicated. On the other hand, maybe it really happened for the best.

God was gracious, though, and kept working in our lives. Our oldest daughter, Samantha, had come to Christ at age four. One night, when she was eleven (Clementine was six), Lalla and I had a meeting to attend at the church, which was only five minutes away from our house. We had never left the girls alone, but decided to this time as the meeting was for only an hour and we were close by. I told Samantha that they should wrap up dinner, clean the kitchen, finish a movie they were watching, and then for some reason, I told her to use the Billy Graham tract *Steps to Peace with God* and lead her sister to Christ! Mostly, I just wanted to keep them busy and free from worry until we returned.

She said OK and we left. We returned and I anxiously queried Samantha about the evening.

"Did you do what I asked?" I said.

"Yes, Dad, of course," she responded. "We did everything you said. We cleaned the kitchen and watched the rest of the movie and then I read the tract to Clementine and she accepted Jesus Christ."

Amazing! This is a great wonder to me to this day. After that, you could always ask Clementine when she came to know Jesus Christ and she would tell you her sister led her to Christ at the age of six. Praise God!

Five years later, however, our family fell apart. Lalla and I divorced. I won't go into all the details, which are unnecessary. I believe multiple factors contributed to it. Suffice it to say that the seeds of problems in our marriage had been sown even before we were married (and before we both came to Christ), when Lalla and I got involved while I was still married to Linda.

During my marriage to Lalla, I genuinely wanted to be the Christian man, husband, and father that God had called me to be, and that my wife needed me to be. I realized years later that I prioritized my daughters above her, though, and she knew it. In addition, I had unresolved physical issues resulting from all of the years I abused my body with drugs and alcohol. That took a toll on us.

Samantha and Clementine were devastated emotionally by the divorce, and in absolute confusion. They went to live with their mom. We didn't know it immediately, but Samantha started drinking and drugging. Her life spiraled downhill. Clementine was only ten at the time, and didn't immediately show the same outward signs, but she was just as affected.

These were exceedingly tough times for me. I had lost my wife, my children, my home, my business partner (Lalla), and my business. I had lost all that mattered to me on this earth, and in grief and depression I simply didn't want to go on living. But God lives His life through others as well. A friend, bible study teacher and mentor at Second Baptist, Don Carpenter, counseled me throughout the divorce and those very hard times. I remember all to the times I called him, despondent and sad, and he would encourage me through my depression and heart break. I can credit Don for helping keep me alive. So again, I was witnessing the body of Christ at work. Another guy in a baseball cap. I am so glad we have a Savior, a Rescuer, a Redeemer who saves us from ourselves.

# Chapter 16

My Story: Closing In On the Work God Prepared

I continued at Second Baptist. I couldn't be involved in ministry at that point, of course due to my recent divorce. But the single parent's bible study class proved to be a great support, and so did a 12-week divorce recovery seminar I took twice (and later helped lead).

I didn't like being single. I started dating women that I met through Christian online dating sites. I was looking for a new wife.

On one occasion, in 1999, I hopped in my Ford Explorer and drove to Austin to meet a lady. In those days I never used a seat belt (typical with my mindset!). But halfway to Austin, I happened to stop for coffee and saw a policeman looking at me. When I got back on the road, I put on my seat belt. About an hour later, some animal crossed the road in front of me. I swerved, lost control of the car, careened across the grass highway median and the opposite two lanes, rolled the car several times, and finally stopped in an open ditch. My car windows were broken out and my belongings from the car were strewn along a hundred-yard stretch. I felt myself to make sure I still had all of my limbs and wasn't bleeding profusely.

At that point I heard a voice clearly.

"If you don't start using the gifts I have given you, I will take them away and I might very well take you out as well."

There has never been a question in my mind that this was God speaking to me. It was very clear and I understood the message. I knew it was time for me to get back into ministry and get serious about my role in expanding the kingdom for Christ.

Two years later, at age 61, I married Vickie Dacus. She had been married once before and had no children. She was twenty years younger than me, and it's amazing she agreed to my proposal, but God has greatly blessed our marriage for these 19 years.

In retrospect, it's obvious to me that when my marriage to Lalla broke up, I was floundering and lost interest in most things important to me. In addition to the grief I was carrying, I disliked being on my own all the time and realized I needed a partner. God gave me Vickie just in time. Strangely, I had been all over the world visiting ladies I met on Christian dating websites, while Vickie was at my Bible study class back at Second Baptist Houston all along. We courted for a while and married.

At that point things began to take off. I had a partner and God's plan for me began to come together. At the time Vickie and I married, I had finally picked up my long-delayed bachelor's degree. The year in college at age 60 caused me to realize I could write and that helped relaunch my pipeline consulting business. I had a growing sense of purpose, because I needed to be a provider and leader for Vickie and to love her well. She was a genuinely loving wife, and for me she was a life-changer. She was the catalyst for moving into the final preparation for God's calling on my life and the work of prison evangelism. Vickie was sent to me by God to give me the structure, responsibility, encouragement, discipline and commitment to carry through with the plans he had for me and us. This last quarter of my life was when it was going to happen and Vickie was my designated partner! A man needs a partner—especially a man in ministry—and she was perfect for me! During this time, I matured enough to start believing that God still had a plan for me, and I started developing steps to carry out that plan.

Vickie and I started doing a lot of ministry together at Second Baptist Houston, in the prayer ministry, co-leading a Sunday morning class with my mentor Jim DeLoach, and doing new member counseling. That was where I had already shared the gospel so many times with people who wanted to join the church. God had called me to evangelize, and I was back at evangelizing. I thank God for giving me Vickie as a partner and getting me on track to accomplish his purpose! Without her, I doubt it would have happened.

In addition, not long after we got married, Vickie and I sought out more systematic training in the things that God first revealed to me in the vision I had in Alaska. God was honing in on the things that He wanted me to be able to communicate effectively:

- Jesus is God in the flesh. He died for our sins and rose from the dead and offers forgiveness to all who put their trust in Him. (John 1:14; 1 Corinthians 15:3-4; Ephesians 1:7; 2:8-9)

- When we put our trust in Christ we are actually born of God. He births a new spirit within us. Our old man dies on the cross with Christ. We are raised a new man. We have a completely new identity. (John 1:13; 3:5; Romans 6:6; Colossians 2:12; 2 Corinthians 5:17)

- Jesus Himself comes to live within us, not to help us live the Christian life, but to live His very own life through us. (Galatians 2:20)

All of these experiences sharing the gospel, and all of the evangelism training I had received, caused me to start experimenting with how best to share the message. It was trial and error. God was training me. I discovered what were effective ways to share the gospel, and what weren't. I would look at some of the materials I was using, and I would think, "This is the most important message this person will ever hear. And I'm sharing it with him in a very abbreviated, five-minute form with stick figures. I think we can do better than that."

In addition to counseling people who came forward at the church, I had been taking people from AA to lunch, developing a relationship with them, and sharing the gospel with them. I would sketch little drawings for them on a yellow legal pad. The idea began to form within me, "I need to have something more substantial to leave with people." That was in 2008. Over time, that idea became the *How to Be a Child of God* booklet.

What I wanted was a resource that would present to people the whole gospel, just as God had done for me. It's wonderful to tell people that Jesus died for their sins, was resurrected, and that by trusting in Him they could get their sins forgiven and Be with Him forever. But that's only half of the gospel: Jesus died *for* us.

Transparency is clear sight with no obstructions. It is the practice of rigorous or total honesty. You often know when a spouse, friend, child, or relative has wronged you or possibly deceived or lied to you. You already know it, but you would like to hear that person acknowledge the deception or wrongdoing. It makes things right and directs all parties toward a more trusting relationship. God sees confession in this same way.

We accumulate a lot of junk. God knows it all and is waiting for us to acknowledge our short-comings. He wants total honesty from His children. He wants us to surrender our old ways and follow Him.

"**B**ut if we confess our sins to him, he is faithful and just to forgive us our sins and to cleanse us from all wickedness (unrighteousness)." 1 John 1:9

* * *

Confession, surrender, and submission are all terms that describe coming to a place where we know that our own plans and our own strength are not enough. We make up our minds to return to God's plan and totally trust Jesus and rely on Him for everything. He literally becomes Lord, God, and Savior to us. Confessing our faults and shortcomings is the first step of acceptance and surrender and coming to the end of self.

Be Specific

It is easiest to say, "I am sorry for all of my sins," in a general way, but God wants you to be personal and specific. The object of Christian growth and development is to have a personal relationship with Jesus Christ and to speak to Him on an intimate and personal basis. Being vague isn't intimate or

11

Walking in the reality of Christ in us.

I wanted to communicate the other half of the gospel as well. Jesus took us to the cross with Him, we died with Jesus, we were raised as completely new creations, with a completely new identity, and Jesus Himself has come to live in us, to live His very life through us. We can live by faith, trusting Him to do that, trusting that He in us is completely sufficient to live the life that only He is capable of living.

That is what God showed me when He gave me the vision of being crucified with Christ. What happened to Him, happened to me. I was completely new, and Jesus was the one living in and through me now.

Drug treatment centers, including Hazelden, teach that unresolved conflicts with our parents are the underlying cause of the vast majority of our problems. That probably overstates it, because we are born into the world sinners, and as a result we can make plenty of our own problems. But there is truth in that statement. The truth is we need a new family—the family of God.

The wonderful thing about being born of God is that, in the depths of my being, I am not the child of Sherrod and LaVella Howell anymore. I am the child of the God of the universe. The Holy Spirit gave birth to me (John 3:5). *The Father brought me forth* (James 1:18). *I am from Him. My new man is created in His likeness, in true holiness and righteousness* (Ephesians 4:24).

This is the rest that God calls us to: laying aside our own efforts at trying hard to be a good Christian and live the Christian life perfectly, and instead walking by faith, trusting that Christ is our life, and that He in us doesn't have to *try hard* to do anything!

I wanted another resource that would communicate all of this. In other words, I wanted a resource that God would use not only to get people through the door of the kingdom, but to teach them from the start to walk in the full reality of that kingdom, the reality of Christ in us.

But it had to be simple. As I've said, I'm a simple kind of guy, and I learned early on that people relate to simple. You start throwing around a bunch of theological terms that church people like to use, and people's eyes start to glaze over. Jesus understood reality better than anyone who has ever walked on this planet, and He didn't throw around a bunch of fancy theological terms like "propitiation" or "substitutionary death on the cross." He said, *"I am the life; come to Me and I will give you life."* And people came.

(I am not saying good theology is unimportant. It is very important. Most of the church needs to upgrade theirs to focus on the message God gave Paul, which is Christ in us! I'm simply talking about how we communicate to people who are being drawn to Christ.)

What God had shown me shortly after I got saved was simple. It was profound, but it was simple. I was crucified with Christ. I was buried with Him. I was raised with Him. My old self was gone. I was a new self. Not only had the sin issue between me and God been completely taken care of, but who I had been in the depths of my being—a sinner in rebellion against God—had been taken care of as well. That guy died, I was completely forgiven, and I was raised a completely new creation.

At this point, as I contemplated developing this resource, I was 68. I had been a Christian 24 years. And I was on the verge of entering into the work that God had prepared for me to do.

About that, of course, I had no clue.

Chapter 17

God Is Not in a Hurry

The truth is that God isn't in the crash course business. He is working with eternity in mind. If He takes 70 years to make it evident what your primary life work is going to be, like He did to me, so what?

Moses was 80 when he started the work God had planned for him all along. Apparently, it took that long to get him to the place where he was ready. He certainly wasn't ready at age 40 when he murdered an Egyptian. He was on the same page with God in wanting to be the deliverer of his people, but he was trying to do it his own way, in his own strength and effort. That was pointless. It was a superhuman task, and it took a superhuman God to do it. All Moses could be was the vessel that said, "I'm willing." At age 80, God had him ready.

The wonderful thing is that God can take anybody, anytime, anywhere and use them for whatever He wants to do. In my case, He took this old drunk roughneck from South Texas and got over a million booklets into prisons, which probably got passed around and at least looked at by five million or so inmates.

Who would have looked at my life at age 40 and predicted it? I was a basket case when I finally surrendered at AA at age 41. But God knew what He was doing. I'm nobody special. I mean, I'm special to God, of course. All of His children are. But I'm just an ordinary guy, no better than anyone else, and worse than most! But He was willing to come live inside me—me!—and express His own life through me to the world. What a God! What a Savior!

I found that God didn't seem to be in a hurry, either, in producing *How to be a Child of God.* The journey from concept to product in hand took a very long time.

I tried to hire a couple of writers to put the text together for me, but I ended up writing it thing myself. God, I discovered, had laid this message on my heart to share, and I was the one best suited to share it.

He does that with all of us. There is the eternal truth of the gospel of Jesus Christ that never changes, but He gives it to each of us in a unique way. We have our own spin on how to share it, and I had to be true to the way He had given me to share.

What I couldn't do myself was illustrate it, and illustrations were key to the whole package. I wanted people to be able to see the reality of the gospel. After all, for most of the last 2,000 years, the gospel has gone out to people who couldn't even read. That's what all those stained-glass etchings were for in those grand cathedrals in the Middle Ages. People couldn't read, so they put the gospel into pictures in church windows.

I understood that a picture is worth a thousand words, so the more pictures, the fewer words to read. I wanted someone to be able to pick up this booklet, look at the pictures, read the simple story, and say,

> *I get it. My real problem isn't that I do bad things. So trying to clean my act up isn't going to help. My real problem is that I'm dead. I'm dead to God. There's only one solution: I need life. Jesus is the life. He is life itself. I need to receive Jesus into myself. Once I have the Son, I have the life. Forever.*

I had to go through several artists before I finally landed on one that grasped what I really wanted to communicate. He was a reformed New Age hippie stoner (okay, a former pothead) named Randy Rodgers, who had come to Jesus years before.

I said to him, "I want to show that this guy in the booklet, this Everyman, is actually placed into Christ, and everything that happens to Christ happens to him. And I want to show that Jesus actually comes to live inside this guy, and that he isn't really the one living this life anymore; it's actually Jesus living in him. Jesus is in him, loving, serving, listening, sharing, being the life that others so desperately need."

Jesus also came so that you and I could have peace and an abundant life on this earth now through a relationship with Him. He wants to show us how to cope with life's problems. Jesus offers hope and a new design for living. Our natural ways keep us self-absorbed and in turmoil. They have not worked.

9   John 10:10, Romans 6:16, Romans 6:21, Romans 8:37, Ephesians 2:14, Revelation 3:20

Simple illustrations.

Randy understood. He started producing simple, life-changing illustrations that anyone could understand—the illustrations you've been seeing throughout this book.

Randy drew the illustrations, we put a prototype together, and I ran it by probably 200 people to get their input—everyone from pastors and teachers to recovered drunks and addicts . We revised it, revised it some more, and produced some final copies. The end product was a four-color booklet 50 pages long, 8.5 by 5.5 inches (the height and width of a full paperback).

God had prepared me all along to produce this booklet. And He had prepared me to get it into the hands of those he intended.

If God has prepared good works beforehand for us to do, then He knows perfectly well what those good works will be and what we will need to do them. To me, nothing could be more obvious about my life than that.

I can just imagine a conversation in heaven between Jesus and an angel forty years ago, shortly before I put my faith in Christ. Years before, Jesus had put the angel in charge of watching over me. The angel had pulled me out of the fire so many times that he had lost count.

"This guy David Howell—he thinks he's so smart," the angel comments. "All his life he's put himself in danger, got himself in horrible messes, and he thinks he's such a slick operator. He can get himself out of any fix. He has no idea that I've been watching over him all these years, guarding him, saving him from himself."

Jesus smiles. "Thank you for serving him like that."

"What's so special about this guy?"

"They're all special."

"But where is all of this going? What, if anything, are you going to do with him? Do you actually want me to keep protecting him?"

And Jesus says, "I'm going to use him to reach millions of prison inmates with the gospel."

"Millions?" The angel replies. "Of inmates? I can imagine him being in prison again, but he's not even one of yours yet."

"Well, that's about to change. And I'll use all those times he's been in jail."

"But he's lived such a hellish life."

"So have all those people in prison."

"But he doesn't even know how to share the gospel."

"I'll give him the gift of evangelism."

"He'll be completely untrained."

"I'll put him in the best training spot. He'll be an evangelism counselor for a Billy Graham crusade, working one-on-one with people. I'll even put him on the leadership team."

The angel shakes his head. "But leadership—that'll be ten years down the road."

"No, I'll do it within a year."

"A year! They'll never put a brand-new Christian in that position."

"Just watch."

"He'll need more training that just one crusade."

"He's going to take every evangelism course around. And counsel people every week at his church with the gospel."

"No churches in Alaska are big enough to need that," the angel points out.

"Churches in Houston are. I'll run thousands of people by him at Second Baptist Church in Houston, ready to hear the gospel."

"But all he's going to know to tell people is Jesus died to forgive their sins."

"No, he's going to know a whole lot more than that. He's going to know that I've joined him to Myself, that he's one with Me, that he died with Me, and now I live through him. I'm going to show him the whole thing."

"And you think he'll be able to share that with others."

"He'll get trained."

"But will prisoners be able to grasp that?"

Jesus nods. "Anyone can grasp that. The gospel isn't complicated.

Besides, David is a simple person. Why do you think I had him born in South Texas and working on oil rigs and running around with roughnecks? He'll know how to communicate simply."

"So how is one guy going to get the gospel to millions of prisoners?"

"Through print."

"Print? How's he going to get that many copies of the gospel into print?"

"He'll publish. Why do you think I taught him all those years to be a publisher?"

"Prisoners don't read. They only have fifth-grade educations."

"He'll communicate at a fifth-grade level. He's good at that."

"No one's going to want to read a boring little booklet," the angel objects.

"It won't be boring. It'll be attractive. Illustrated. Great illustrations."

"David doesn't draw."

"He knows how to find people that do. He's a publisher."

"But how's he going to get these into prisons?"

"Mail," Jesus replies.

"Mail? To thousands of prisons?"

"Why do you think I taught him how to do mass mail marketing campaigns?"'

"He can't mail books to anonymous prisoners."

"They'll go to chaplains. He knows how to relate to decision-makers. Why do you think I've been teaching him to do that all these years?"

"But he won't have enough money. It'll be expensive. He'll use his money to retire."

"He won't retire. I'll keep bringing him business deals to fund the whole thing."

"Into his 70s?" the angel asks.

"Into his 80s."

"Into his 80s? There's no way he's going to live that long. Not the way he's treated his body."

"We're going to turn that around. I'm going to show him how to treat his body right, and I'm going to bring healing. He'll be around a long time."

"But . . . he's so . . . flawed."

Jesus laughs. "So true! But I am perfect, and I'm the one who lives in him. Watch and see what I can do."

Over the years, the angel watched. "This isn't going anywhere," the angel would say. "It's just a big mess."

Jesus would smile. "Just watch."

And then, one day, the angel saw. He saw the whole tapestry that Jesus had been weaving, and the good work He was now accomplishing, and he was amazed.

Just like I've been amazed.

Chapter 18

The Nuts and Bolts

The responses I get to *How to be a Child of God* show me that, dollar for dollar, this is the most effective evangelism ministry I've heard of. Based on inmate feedback, I estimate that at least ten percent of the inmates who read it get saved. Probably many more than that, but that's a conservative estimate. I've learned that about a third of the prisoners will have an interest in the booklet. So that's how many I send. If it's a 900-person prison, I'll send 300 booklets. Even if only 10% of those 300 accept Christ, that's 30 people added to God's kingdom.

Including 250,000 Spanish language booklets, as of December 2020, we've distributed over 1.1 million copies. So, that's over 100,000 people added to God's kingdom. It's just an estimate, but probably a decent one. The cost for those million booklets has been $500,000. So it's costing $5 for every person who comes to Christ. That's the most cost-effective evangelism ministry I've ever heard of, at least in America. Maybe they can do evangelism cheaper in Africa.

The reason it's so effective, of course, is that the harvest is so ripe in prisons. These are men and women whose lives have fallen apart. *They are in prison!* They are at the end of themselves. They look at their lives and they admit, "All my best thinking and planning has landed me in this prison cell for the next five years. Maybe I need to reevaluate what life is all about." Their situation is miserable, and, though they may not admit it, so many have lost all hope for the future. As far as they know, they have little or no future, even when they get released.

Then they hear people talking about Jesus, or someone hands them a copy of *How to Be a Child of God*. And they think, "Maybe I should

CÓMO SER

...Un Hijo De

Dios

Edición para Testificar
Incluye: *Cómo contar tu historia* y **Cómo testificar**

The Spanish version of How to Be a Child of God

actually consider this." They hear the message that God will not only forgive them, He will completely change them on the inside, and He Himself will come to live in them, giving them new life. It is a life-changing message, and inmate after inmate responds to it.

The people around me and you every day, the people outside of prison, still have hope that they can make life work. We all still have a free will, so to speak. We can pursue whatever we want to in life. Usually, people out here aren't as desperate, aren't as hungry. They have too many distractions that compete for their attention. Men and women in prison have lost their free will. They have to do whatever the warden tells them to do. And they certainly don't have too many distractions to keep their mind off the realities of life.

It's a field ripe for harvest. God knows that.

I say to people, "Find me another mission field in America where one-third of the audience actually wants to sit down and read through a 50-page book explaining the gospel, and where over ten percent of those who read it will put their faith in Christ, on their own. You can't."

It's a thrill knowing I'm doing what I'm supposed to do and God is doing through me what He wants done. Pretty soon I had the whole operation streamlined. I had a printer that could print mass quantities of *How to Be a Child of God* for 50 cents apiece. I had the mailing list of all the prisons, which I provided to my printer. I had a FedEx account that the printer could use to deliver them.

(All of God's preparation of me, teaching me how to do direct mail mass marketing, paid off tremendously.)

I can literally pick up the phone, make one call to the printer, tell them, as I did just the other day, "Please print 100,000 new copies and send them to these prisons in these quantities," and it's done.

I developed a rotating system of sending each prison all the books they could use every two and a half years. Approximately 80 to 90 percent of inmates are in and out of the penitentiary in that amount of time, so sending new books to the prisons every two and a half years puts them in the hands of a whole new set of people. I cover one region of the country, and a few months later I do the next region.

I employ one lady part-time who updates the mailing list, maintains databases, and handles other details. The whole thing is a two-person part-time operation, plus our donors who make it happen.

Printing quantities of *Seeking God Through Prayer and Meditation* are much smaller, so the price per book is higher. I typically print 5,000 of those at a time for two or three dollars apiece. It costs $2.25 to mail it. So, for $5 or under, I can send an inmate high-quality material by which he can be discipled, and a 30-day devotional that he can go through 12 times a year if he chooses to.

Where does the money come from to do all of this? Well, God. He sends some—30% maybe—through people who hear about the ministry. Mostly through a few faithful donors. Some inmates whose lives have been changed are able to contribute after they get out and start making it on their own. That's always a thrill, to see a former inmate want to be involved in passing on the gospel that way. A few start contributing while they are in prison! The main ones who understand how ripe the harvest is in prisons are ex-cons. They know it. God does, too.

I've tried to raise money from countless churches and foundations. I've hired public relations guys. I've done dozens of radio interviews. I've been on the *700 Club* TV show. I've asked all the big Christian publishers to publish *How to Be a Child of God*, so they could foot the bill. None of it ever yielded much—and I'm a pretty good marketer.

God seems to have had other plans. I always figured I would have retired from business long before now. But here I am at age 81, and God is still bringing oilfield pipe deals for me to be involved in, and they make good money. The business He keeps giving me is what primarily funds the ministry. Sometimes an unlikely deal happens, and I think, "God really wants these books distributed."

If I had had my way, I would have had this ministry make a big splash and be over all sorts of media and the money would have come pouring in. I would have retired and lived as a ministry president and just encouraged the people doing the work!

But that was never God's way. God chose to get the gospel to all of these people—precious in His sight—and, for this specific ministry, I'm the instrument He chose to live through. There was never to be a dime in this for me. As long as I'm the ministry's benefactor, not its benefiter, He blesses it. It was all to be for the people who receive the gospel. That's the way Jesus is. He lays down His life for others. He did that completely while He was on earth, and now He lives in those who are His. He still lays down His life. He does it through us. We get the joy of seeing others blessed.

How do the prisoners get a hold of the booklets? Large county jails (and some prisons) have sitting rooms, TV rooms, and libraries. Inmates can pick them up there. In places where those areas aren't available, prison workers often go by with carts and inmates can pick a book. Then, of course, they pass them around to each other.

My real heart is for the books to get to the people in prison who are truly all alone. I say to chaplains, "Give these to people who are in administrative segregation, in isolation." Regular prison ministries can go into prisons and have rallies and prayer meetings and Bible studies, which is great. I supply books to a hundred or so of those ministries and they can hand them out there, too. But only the prisoners with good behavior can come to those events. The ones not on good behavior, who are simply forced to sit in their cells day after day, those are the ones I most want to reach. They don't have a smartphone or access to a TV. They have nothing. You give them

Dear, Mr. Howell;   4/16/19

Hello, Sir. My name is ████████████████████, and I'm currently serving a life sentence in the state of Georgia.

Sir, I just wanted to thank you PERSONALLY for even taking the time to distribute something like "How To Be A Child Of God". People such as myself are rarely told that they still matter — or can still be somebody....

If you're wondering what I mean when I say, "people such as myself", I mean this: I'm currently located in a special part of the prison called "The Tier II Program". The only time I'm allowed out of my cell is to shower and for medical emergencies. And for the most part, I'm pretty healthy. So that leaves showers only....

But I say all of that, to say this; people like me are EASILY forgotten.... So for you to take the time to distribute something like "How To Be A Child Of God"... I really appreciate it. May God Bless You....

Hopefully, you don't mind if we correspond. I don't have much family, and all of my friends are gang-members. If I was able to, I'd be more than happy to attend a few of the prison church services, but this prison doesn't have a chaplain — and I'm rarely allowed out of my cell. I still don't understand how Christian Fellowship can be considered a privilege for inmates who "behave" (it's the ones like me who need it the most), but that's the situation I'm in. So regular correspondence with someone who's willing to hold my hand through this Christian-Walk thing would really be appreciated.... Thank you for your time and patience;

Sincerely,

How to Be a Child of God and they will read it over and over. I know, because they tell me. And as they read it repeatedly, the message sinks in.

What a joy, to be able to bring the message of new life in Christ to someone like that. I'm the guy in the booklet in the baseball hat, just like everyone else. Just an ordinary guy. God can take anybody, anytime, anywhere, and use them for whatever He wants to do. That's why Christ lives in us, to live His life through us, to bring life to a dead and dying world.

I discovered that God has such a heart for prisoners. When He first proclaimed His ministry, Jesus, quoting Isaiah, said He had come to set the prisoners free (Luke 4:18). Certainly, that means setting free all of us who lived in spiritual prison, but He meant it literally, too. God wants to set free those who are in prison. He tells us to remember the prisoners (Hebrews 13:3). Paul himself spent a significant part of his ministry in prison, proclaiming the gospel there. God's love and the good news of Jesus Christ are for prisoners!

For the most part, God has laid on my heart to spread the gospel to prisoners in America. I put 1,000 books in a Columbian prison, but my first priority, at least in print, is evangelizing U.S. prisons. Of course, God never puts His work in a box. *How to Be a Child of God* has been translated and put online as an ebook in 30 different languages at this point. Russian, Mandarin, Burmese, Thai, Vietnamese, you name it. People can download them and share them for free. The online translations have over a million views. (See–HowToBeAChildOfGod.com.)

We also have a YouTube video of the book. It's 21 minutes long and is in English, Spanish, and Portuguese. Together, these have over 200,000 views. When we first did the Russian ebook, somehow a missionary or someone in some little village got hold of it. It got passed to other villages, and within a week 700 or so villages were lit up with it on Google analytics in Siberia and nearby. That was a delight to see.

In addition, we have produced two Facebook pages, "*How to Be a Child of God*" and "Prison Evangelism Inc." The first is visited primarily by people apart from prison, all over the world. People post their reactions to the booklet. Often, it's obvious that they are already sold-out Christians.

The second Facebook page, "Prison Evangelism Inc.," primarily gets visited by people associated with prisoners. Postings on that one are filled with pictures of tattoos and language full of profanity. That's just the way they talk, at least until God shows them a better

Say with your mouth and believe in your heart that Jesus died, was buried, and came back to life. Trust in Him that He is Lord, Savior and God in the flesh and become a Child of God and co-heir with Christ.

John 11:25-26, John 14:6-7, Romans 10:9, Romans 10:13, 1 Corinthians 6:17, Ephesians 1:5-8, Ephesians 2:8-10, Colossians 2:6-7, 1 John 5:12-13

15

way. I know. I was the same way until God took that out of my life! Praise God that He reaches down and touches the lives of raw people like me, making us whole and alive through His Spirit.

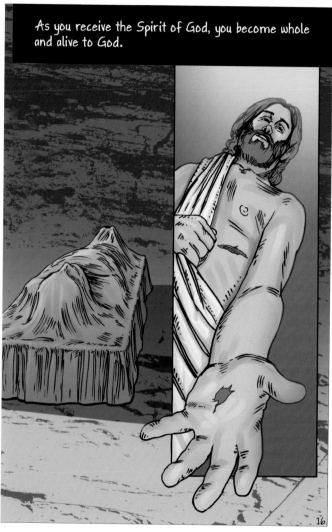

As you receive the Spirit of God, you become whole and alive to God.

The good news is for prisoners!

Chapter 19

God's Workmanship

I look back over my life and it's so clear to me how God orchestrated everything to accomplish what He wanted to accomplish, to live through me in the way He wanted to live through me. That's why this isn't really a story about David Howell at all. It's a story about God, and His heart for millions of people who need to hear the good news of Jesus Christ, and how He chose to bring that good news to them. It's a story about work He has planned to do in the world from before time.

I'm simply a vessel that He chose to prepare, equip, and use. Jesus is the one who lives in me. He has done it.

Jesus does that with all of us who are His. We are His body, His arms and legs on earth. Paul takes that truth just about as far as it will go. He says that we and Jesus are actually one:

> But the one who joins himself to the Lord is one spirit with Him. (1 Corinthians 6:17)

Not only that, but He says that we, as His body, are actually *part* of Christ.

> For even as the body is one and yet has many members, and all the members of the body, though they are many, are one body, so also is Christ. (1 Corinthians 12:12)

Paul isn't saying that we become God, of course. But he goes to great lengths to explain to us the incredible depths of our union with Christ, and the reality of Him living through us.

Our role is to be absolutely and totally surrendered to Jesus Christ. His desire is to live His life in us and through us in order to accomplish His purpose on this earth.

We literally are the Body of Christ, and He desires to use each of us to reach others and expand the Family Welcome to the Family of God. You are a new creature! Say "good-bye" to the old self and "hello" to the new self, with Jesus Christ living in you.

Romans 6:11-13, Romans 8:10, Romans 12:1, Romans 12:4-5,
1 Corinthians 3:16, 1 Corinthians 6:19-20, 2 Corinthians 5:16-21,
Ephesians 4:21-24, Philippians 2:5-8, Colossians 1:27,
1 John 3:1-3, 1 John 3:9-10, 1 John 5:18-19

25

We are His body. Jesus lives in us and through us.

Sometimes a friend will say to me, "David, you're taking this Jesus in you stuff too far!" I reply, "Hey, I'm not the one who takes it that far. Paul is." To the Corinthians he got really practical:

Do you not know that your bodies are members of Christ? Shall I then take away the members of Christ and make them members of a prostitute? May it never be! (1 Corinthians 6:15)

Jesus is living in us even when we do things completely contrary to Him. He may be holding His nose the whole time, but He is right there in it with us. He doesn't go anywhere.

Praise God, though, that He is at work in us, so we will choose and fulfill His good purposes for us (Philippians 2:13). That is our true heart now, to please Him, to glorify Him, to be a vessel for His use.

God has given us a sphere of influence for a reason. It may be big. It may be small. The size is His business. He knows exactly what He is doing, and what He intends to accomplish.

Prisoners who come to Christ often have a sphere of influence only extending to the guy in the next cell. That's it, at least while they're in prison. That's where God wants to use them. Letting God use them might simply mean passing along a booklet or sending it home to a child or grandchild. Maybe you have a sphere of influence about that size. That's where God wants to use you.

In the second part of *How to Be a Child of God*, I teach the reader how to tell someone their testimony. I think it's so important for us to be able to tell someone, "This is where I was in life, and then Jesus intervened, and here's what God has done for me." It doesn't have to be anything fancy. But it's important to be able to do it.

I have found that when a person comes to know Jesus Christ and realizes he has a new life, he immediately becomes excited about it and wants to share with whomever will listen. He wants to tell what happened to him! But new believers need to be taught how to witness. It doesn't require a long, involved course in evangelism (though those can be useful). The easiest way for believers to witness is to tell their story of how it was, what happened, and how it is now after they have come to know Jesus. If we wait to instruct them until they've had time to marinate for a while, and then go through a long evangelism course, it's often too late! They've lost their excitement in telling what happened to them. God wants to use them as His witnesses *now*.

That is why, in *How to Be a Child of God*, we put the information

I was blind, and now I can see! John 9:25

How to Tell Your Story
Christian Witness through Personal Testimony

Sharing your personal testimony of coming to know and trust Jesus Christ is the first step in practicing personal evangelism. There are two types of personal testimony. One is historical, which is telling about your life before, during and after the time you came to trust Jesus Christ as Lord and God, and Savior of your soul. The other is a theme type testimony and might simply be the event of your salvation and what life has been like since that time. This could be for someone who came to Christ as a child and might report of his life since conversion. Another example could be a person who had believed he was a Christian all his life but found he really didn't know God and then came to the point of surrender and repentance.

BEGIN THE TESTIMONY BY MENTIONING SOME COMMON GROUND YOU AND YOUR SUBJECT SHARE; SAME HOMETOWN, SAME JOB, SAME SCHOOL, ETC. FIND SOME MUTUAL INTERESTS.

33

Simple witnessing

about telling one's story and witnessing immediately following the sinner's prayer. With this information, the newly saved can learn how to simply tell his story and use that story and the witness teaching that follows to lead others to Christ. A prison unit is like a community where people eat, sleep, work, and play. They also communicate in groups of like interests. It's an ideal setting for evangelism! Providing simple instruction works very well for spreading the gospel inside prison walls.

A certain percentage of these newly saved find they have the gift of evangelism. The excitement stays with this bunch and, if given direction up front when they receive Christ, they can lead a lot of people to Christ!

If people receive just basic training in how to tell the story of what Christ has done for us in His death and resurrection, and what God has done in their lives personally, it's amazing the impact they can have, especially in a prison setting. People who are incarcerated have all the time in the world. When God makes their hearts receptive to hearing a spiritual message, they will take the time to listen.

Often, allowing God to use us requires that we get out of our holy huddles. Hanging around other believers is easy. It's comfortable. But it's not where the people who need life are! Jesus didn't just hang around the disciples all the time. Far from it.

We often think we've blown it too badly for God to use us. Nonsense. I had a whole lifetime of blowing it badly. I still do! Do we really think that God didn't know how badly we were going to mess up? We are the ones He has chosen to live in, and use for His purposes. He has made us qualified to share in His inheritance (Colossians 1:13). Who are we to tell Him that we are unqualified?

We aren't liabilities to God. We are His precious assets. He has freely chosen to come live in us, because that is where He wants to live. He knew we wouldn't be perfect. He chose to live in us and through us anyway. Let's let Him.

Since putting my faith in Christ, I haven't had 100% victory in every area of my life. Have you? Okay, then, we're all on the same page. Now we can get on with God.

God showed me that at the cross, we are *completely* forgiven. The sin issue between us and God has been *completely* removed. Jesus came to put away sin (Hebrews 9:26), and that He did! God has done everything He needed to do to make us the vessels He wants to use. We are vessels who still blow it sometimes. Fine. Jesus took care of that. He is still living in us, living through us, as we trust Him to do it (Galatians 2:20). Let's move forward, tell God we are His vessel for His use, and get on with the task. He is the one who is at work in us and through us. All He asks us to do is be willing.

The truth is that God will use anyone who is willing. We often let our pride and ego and self-made plans get in the way. We think we know what's best for us, what we want. God's agenda is so much bigger than that. The one who lives in us was never about pleasing Himself (Romans 15:3). He was about being available to the Father. He was about laying down His life that others might be blessed. He is still that way in us today.

In my case, God took this drunk, simple roughneck from South Texas who for his first 43 years lived a hellish life. He gave me the parents He wanted, with all of their shortcomings, and the upbringing I needed. Through my very imperfect dad, He taught me to be determined, to persist and not give up. That has served me well.

God taught me to have a business sense, taught me how to spot opportunities, taught me to put together marketing material, and to publish, and to do mass mail marketing, all before I even came to Christ. He taught me how to relate to prisoners—by continually letting me get thrown in jail! He taught me to relate to Hispanics, and to love Hispanic culture, because He knew many of the people He wanted to reach through me would be Hispanic (as well as other cultures).

At the time, I thought all of these things (the good ones, at least) were for my sake, to help make my life more pleasant. I was wrong.

After I came to Christ, He gave me the gift of evangelism, and trained me to be an evangelist through some of the top evangelism ministries in the world. He had me share the gospel one on one with several thousand people, taking me through trial and error, figuring out what people responded to and what they didn't.

He took me through some great training on the reality of what happened to us when God birthed us, what our true new identity is, and what it means that Christ now lives in us.

Since I had abused my body so badly for decades, God restored my health by teaching me to eat natural foods, go on fasts, and do body cleansings. God knew that the work He had prepared for me would require me to stick around quite a while. I was obedient in these things, and I believe God used them to lengthen my life.

Along the way, God let me go through some unbelievably hard times and personal struggles, because He knew the audience He had for me would go through the same struggles.

The last quarter of my life, He gave me a partner, Vickie, who wanted to grow in experiencing the reality of Christ in us as much as I did.

And, maybe most important, very early in my Christian life, He showed me the reality that He would want me to communicate so clearly 30 years later: that I was one with Christ, that I died with Him, that I was raised with Him, and that He was the one living in and through me.

For the next 30 years, He used me in people's lives, to be sure. But for the most part He was equipping me and preparing me for my real life purpose, the work He wanted to accomplish through me. And He wasn't in a hurry to get me there.

As I said before, the guy in the baseball cap in *How to Be a Child of God* is me, and he is you. He is every one of us that God has called to Himself. We were all sinners, separated from God, trying to make life work on our own. In truth, we were walking corpses. We were dead—dead to God.

But when we placed our trust in Jesus, He came inside us and gave us life. He joined Himself to us and became our life (Colossians 3:4). Now, like the guy in the baseball cap, Jesus Himself lives in us, and through us. We are the vessels of His own life.

And He knows how He plans to live through us.

What a miracle. What a Savior!

Chapter 20

From Ordinary to Extraordinary

In the kind of ministry God has given me, I don't have the luxury of sitting down and talking with each person one on one. If five million people have read the booklets, that would be a lot of conversations. I'm not sure God will keep me here quite that long!

I've had such conversations many times over the years, of course. Thousands of times. Those conversations were meant to draw men and women at those moments to Christ. And, I realize now, God was using them to train me as well, to teach me how to most effectively share not only the message that Christ died for our sins, but the rest of the gospel as well: that Christ has come to live in us, to live His life through us.

The end result of all of that training has been *How to Be a Child of God*, and its follow-up discipleship booklet, *Seeking God Through Prayer and Meditation*. God has blessed those and used them mightily, just like He planned all along.

I'm 81 now, and only God knows how much longer I'll be around to do this ministry, or how much longer God will use me to finance it. I've been laying the groundwork for someone else to carry on the work. The book you are reading is part of that process, to let people know how this ministry got started, how God ordained that He would use me in this way, how God prepared and equipped me, and how God faithfully accomplished what He set out to do.

This truly is God's story. It always has been.

I still enjoy sitting down with people and sharing one on one, whether they have already come to Christ or not. Jesus is the life. People apart from God need to hear that and come to Him. People joined to God already need to understand that and learn to live in the fullness of Christ in them.

At this point, if I could sit down and talk with every man and woman who has come to Christ after reading *How to Be a Child of God*, I would simply tell them this:

> You already have it all, you know. You're complete in Christ. You're not only *accepted* in Christ, you are completely acceptable. There's not one thing you're missing. God has given you Himself, and that's all He can give you. He is the very life within you. He is the love. He is the joy. He is the peace. He is the patience. He is the power. He is the self-control. He is everything you will ever need. You don't need to do a bunch of spiritual stuff to get more of Him. You don't need to jump through a bunch of religious hoops. You have all of Him right now.

> Just grow in receiving that reality. All He wants you to do is say, "Lord, I'm the vessel you have chosen to live in. I make myself completely available to you. You live through me, and love through me, and lay down your life through me, in the all the ways You want to."

> It's a faith walk. That's all it is—a faith walk. You and I are one spirit with Him. We can't get any closer than that. We trust that He speaks to us, that He guides us, that He lives through us, that He does through us exactly the good works He has prepared for us to do. And we glorify Him as we see Him do it.

I've always been an ordinary guy. You've probably always been an ordinary man or woman. We are the kind of people God chooses to use. When Jesus invades a life, joining us to Himself, and comes to live in and through us, that's when the extraordinary starts to happen.

God doesn't measure extraordinary by numbers. He measures it by who's doing it. If He's doing it, it's extraordinary, whether the world sees it as big or as small. And He is doing it, through us.

Jesus calls us to rest in that reality, to trust that He is perfectly able to live His own life in us, and to simply be willing for Him to do it. Then we have the incredible privilege of watching Him do it, and knowing we are the vessels He chooses to live through. That's our hope of seeing God's glory—Christ living in us.

What an amazing gospel. Hallelujah! What an amazing Savior.

If you were sincere in your prayer, you are now a member of a new family -- the Family of God. God the Father adopts us all as His own children, and we become co-heirs with our older brother Jesus. He accepts you and loves you unconditionally as a part of His family YOU ARE A CHILD OF GOD!

Psalm 16:11, Romans 5:11, Romans 8:15-17a, 2 Corinthians 5:17,
Philippians 3:20a, Hebrews 2:11-12, Revelation 21:2

20

God continually adding to His family and kingdom.

Epilogue

By David Gregory
Author of
The New York Times
bestseller
Dinner with a Perfect Stranger

David Howell sent me a copy of *How to Be a Child of God* not long after he first published it. We had run in some of the same circles and he told me how much one of my books had meant to him. I had no idea at that early date how powerfully God would use the resource he had produced in jails and prisons across America and also overseas. When I heard the story of what God had done, I knew it would be an honor to help him put it into print.

There's a reason God has used this resource so mightily, of course. It presents in a uniquely simple way not only the first half of the gospel—that Christ died for our sins and rose again so that, through faith in His name, we can receive forgiveness. It also presents the second half—that we died with Christ, that He raised us to new life, that He birthed within us an entirely new heart, and then He came to live within us, so that He could live His own life through us. People desperately need both halves, especially desperate people, which is what prisoners are.

If you have never entered into a personal relationship with Jesus Christ, the message of *How to Be a Child of*

God, and *Breaking into Prison, is for you.* God loved you so much that He sent his own Son to make that eternal relationship with Him possible. Pages 13 and 14 of How to Be a Child of God shows you how. God wants you to be His child today!

If you have received Christ by faith in the past, but you have struggled to find what you know could be your experience—victory and truly abundant life—these two books are for you as well. Go back through the truths they present. The abundance God has for us doesn't come through trying harder (praise God!); it comes through faith in all that He has already freely given us in Christ (1 Corinthians 2:12 and Galatians 2:20).

Maybe you have made wrong turns in your life (which of us hasn't?) and feel that, as a result, God can't use you in any significant way. If there is one thing David's own story shows, He can, and He will. He will use anyone who is willing to simply be a vessel available to Him. He has prepared good works for you to do (Ephesians 2:10), and through you He will bear fruit that remains (John 15:16).

Breaking into Prison has told the story of Prison Evangelism and its publications, and has celebrated how God is using these publications in prisons across the country and in other languages around the world. These booklets are available in print and online for you to use in your personal evangelism and discipleship ministry. You can access them at prisonevangelism. com and howtobeachildofgod.com.

Prison Evangelism is always seeking to expand its work with God in growing His eternal kingdom by reaching millions more with the message of God's free gift in Christ. If you would like to partner with Prison Evangelism financially or in prayer, they look forward to hearing from you at prisonevangelism.com. You can also email David Howell at davidhowell@prisonevangelism.com.

"To Him who loves us and released us from our sins by His blood—and He has made us to be a kingdom, priests to His God and Father—to Him be the glory and the dominion forever and ever." (Revelation 1:5-6)

What Prisoners Say About the Books

In the last number of years I have received thousands of cards and letters from incarcerated men and women whose lives have been touched by *How to Be a Child of God, Seeking God Through Prayer and Meditation, and Fully Alive and Finally Free*. In truth, these cards and letters tell the story of God's amazing work better than I ever could. On the following pages are just a few of them.

Helping to Change Lives

IN PRISON BUT NOT IMPRISONED
AN ORIGINAL POEM BY ▮▮▮▮▮▮

I USED TO BE A SLAVE TO SIN
CONSTANTLY FIGHTING THE WAR WITHIN.
THE WORST PLACE TO BE WAS IN MY OWN MIND.
NO REST OR PEACE, NO RELIEF OF ANY KIND.
NOWHERE TO RUN, NO PLACE TO HIDE.
FREE ON THE OUT BUT IN CHAINS INSIDE.
AN INSANE BRAIN, A HEART TORN APART.
I WANTED TO ESCAPE, BUT DIDN'T KNOW WHERE TO START
OUT AND ABOUT, I WAS FREE PHYSICALLY
YET TRAPPED IN A PRISON YOU COULDN'T SEE MENTALLY
HOW BIG IS MY SKULL? THE SIZE OF MY OWN CELL.
WHO COULD I CALL INSIDE MY OWN HELL?
THERE'S ONLY ONE, HE WHO CAN GET THE BLIND TO SEE.
WHILE I FAKE A SMILE TO HIDE THE PAIN INSIDE OF ME
BEAT DOWN AND DEFEATED, BROUGHT TO MY KNEES
TO JESUS I PLEADED, "GOD SAVE ME PLEASE ?!"
WITH HIS GRACE THROUGH FAITH, I WAS SAVED.
FORGIVEN OF ALL MY SINS NO LONGER A SLAVE.
SOMETHING SO SIMPLE, ALL IT TOOK WAS CONFESSION.
THEN JESUS CAME IN, AND HE TOOK MY DEPRESSION.
NO LONGER BOUND BY THE DESIRES OF THE FLESH.
HE SMASHED THE CHAINS HOLDING ME DOWN AND
SAVED ME FROM DEATH.
LIKE JESUS CHRIST, MY SAVIOR, I HAVE BEEN RISEN
FOR THOUGH I'M IN PRISON, I'M NO LONGER
IMPRISONED.

My SON ▮▮▮▮▮▮ ASKED ME TO
MAIL YOU A COPY OF THIS POEM HE
WROTE.

Nancy

Putnamville Correctional
1946 West US 30
Greencastle IN 46135

Helping to Change Lives

I want to dig a little deeper. Please send a free copy of "SEEKING GOD THROUGH PRAYER AND MEDITATION".

Name
Address PO Box 104
City, State, Zip Mobile AL 36601
Mobile Metro Jail 402-C #54

Please tell us what you think of "How To Be A Child Of God". This book has set me free. I have been able to inspire others to read and follow instructions and I know it will change their lives too!

I want to dig a little deeper. Please send a free copy of "SEEKING GOD THROUGH PRAYER AND MEDITATION".

Name
Address 1300 Cherry St.
City, State, Zip Kansas City mo 64130

Please tell us what you think of "How To Be A Child Of God". I loved the book it changed my life. I will recommend this to friends & family. It changed my views on things. I feel it has brought me closer to god. I think this is a great book & will help many people. I feel I have been reborn

---

72019

I want to dig a little deeper. Please sender a free copy of "SEEKING GOD THROUGH PRAYER AND MEDITATION".

Name
Address 904 Fm 686
City, State, Zip Dayton, Tx 77535
Plane State Jail

Please tell us what you think of "How To Be A Child Of God". I love this little book it's changed my life! Thank ya'll so much! I know that I'm in prison but I was just wondering if ya'll might have the full Bible in this comic book form I started reading it in my county but got transferred and had to return it! God Bless!!

Prison Evangelism, Inc. PO Box 571977 Houston Texas 77257

I want to dig a little deeper. Please send a free copy of "SEEKING GOD THROUGH PRAYER AND MEDITATION".

Name
Address Adams County Detention Facility 150 N. 19th Ave.
City, State, Zip Brighton, Colorado 80601-1951

Please tell us what you think of "How To Be A Child Of God". "I was lost, but Now I'm Found," best describes My situation after reading this book. I lost my wife #25½ yrs. last Dec. 20th in "Mt. Vernon, Tx." and since comming up here in Sodom & Gamorra Colorado, I strayed to & Now I'm all alone & ashamed, but reading this book & relearning of God has been my New me wake-up call. (Native Texan) I miss You Howell. Thank you Carl

Prison Evangelism, Inc. 510 Bering Dr. Suite 300 Houston Texas 77057

130   Breaking Into Prison

Helping to Change Lives

(A)

I want to dig a little deeper. Please send a free copy of "SEEKING GOD THROUGH PRAYER AND MEDITATION".

Name _____

Address 300 Corrections Drive

City, State, Zip _____ NewPort ARKansas 72112

Please tell us what you think of "How To Be A Child Of God". It has me thinking That I need to change my way of life and it also shows me That I can leave a big bag of my old life behind and start a new one with god and be his child.

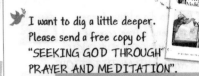

I want to dig a little deeper. Please send a free copy of "SEEKING GOD THROUGH PRAYER AND MEDITATION".

Name _____

Address KilBy Correctional Facility P.O box 15

City, State, Zip MOUNT Meigs, Al 36057-0150

Please tell us what you think of "How To Be A Child Of God". I thought It was very moving an Inspirational and let me Know first exactly what Christ went through. It's been a miraculous Change in my life. I'm also Planting seeds for my Ten special names!

2019

I want to dig a little deeper. Please sender a free copy of "SEEKING GOD THROUGH PRAYER AND MEDITATION".

Name _____

Address Coffield Unit 2661 FM 2054

City, State, Zip Tennessee Colony TX 75884

Please tell us what you think of "How To Be A Child Of God". This Book was instrumental to A change within me. I actually felt the baggage removed from my life as I both read over And saw the Illustrations within. A serious Spiritual Awakening happened with Steven. Close to the same time I read over this teaching I understood what the Great Commission is "Luke 24:44-56" The Lord helped me witness to many prisoners with several copies of this little helpful tool. Praise God for the hands that created it.

Prison Evangelism, Inc.   PO Box 571977   Houston Texas 77257

72019

I want to dig a little deeper. Please sender a free copy of "SEEKING GOD THROUGH PRAYER AND MEDITATION".

Name _____

Address P.O Box 1098

City, State, Zip Burnet County Jail Burnet texas 78611

Please tell us what you think of "How To Be A Child Of God". I think the Book of How to be a child of god is good because it had a big impact on me It really made me wanna change my life and turn my life to god And i wanna say thank you for that.

Prison Evangelism, Inc.   PO Box 571977   Houston Texas 77257

Helping Prisoners Come to Christ

A

🕊 I want to dig a little deeper.
Please send a free copy of
"SEEKING GOD THROUGH
PRAYER AND MEDITATION".

Name
Address A-5-PC-LEWIS-RAST MAX
City, State, Zip P.O. Box 3600
BUCKEYE, AZ. 85326

Please tell us what you think of "How
To Be A Child Of God". Reading
the Child of God made
me realize that when
the guy from Victory Out
reach witnessed to me I
should've listened to what
he told me. Now many years
later my heart + mind
finally accepted Jesus
Christ into my heart and
im finally at peace with
myself.

ison Evangelism, Inc. 510 Bering Dr. Suite 300 Houston Texas 77057

720

🕊 I want to dig a little deeper.
Please sender a free copy of
"SEEKING GOD THROUGH
PRAYER AND MEDITATION".

Name
Address 3600 Havana
City, State, Zip Denver, CO. 80239

Please tell us what you think of "How
To Be A Child Of God". Love this
book very much. I believe
it may be one of my favorit
books. It makes me want
to tell all my friends about
how to be a child of god.
Thank you, because this
book has truely changed
me. Into a child of God.
And help me to want to invite
others to do the same.

---

②?

🕊 I want to dig a little deeper.
Please send a free copy of
"SEEKING GOD THROUGH
PRAYER AND MEDITATION".

Name
Address 21 FM 247
City, State, Zip Huntsville TX.
77320

Please tell us what you think of "How
To Be A Child Of God". I was cleaning
my cell and I came across it
And After looking through it, I
couldn't put it down. I asked for
forgiveness And shortly after I felt
something unbelievable go
through my body, I feel born again
At 50 years old wanting to gain
more, please send anything you can.
Thankyou and God
Bless

rison Evangelism, Inc. 510 Bering Dr. Suite 300 Houston Texas 77057

✓

🕊 I want to dig a little deeper.
Please send a free copy of
"SEEKING GOD THROUGH
PRAYER AND MEDITATION".

Name
Address 1000 Airbase Rd. Pollock
City, State, Zip Pollock LA, 71467 med

Please tell us what you think of "How
To Be A Child Of God". I liked
it a lot. It showed me a
lot of good points. I ask
the Lord to come in my
life today. I'm tired
of being lose. I am found
and not alone any more
Thank you for this book

Prison Evangelism, Inc. 510 Bering Dr. Suite 300 Houston Texas 77057

Helping Prisoners Come to Christ

I want to dig a little deeper. Please send a free copy of "SEEKING GOD THROUGH PRAYER AND MEDITATION".

Name

Address 904 FM 686

City, State, Zip Dayton TX 77535

Please tell us what you think of "How To Be A Child Of God". It was very encaraseno I now have good in my heart and want to share Him with others

, Inc. 510 Bering Dr. Suite 300 Houston Texas 77057

72019

Quiero profundizar un poco más. Por favor envíe una copia gratuita de "BUSCANDO A DIOS A TRAVÉS DE ORACIÓN Y MEDITACIÓN".

Nombre

Dirección 150 N 19th Ave

Ciudad, Estado, Código Brighton CO 80601

Cuéntanos qué te parece "Cómo ser un Hijo de Dios". Me gusto mucho porque habla las verdades de Dios y nuestro Señor Cristo Jesus. Yo leo la biblia diariamente y le doy graciasa Dios por tenerme aqui aunque estoy encarcelado e encontrado a Jesus y eso me a liberado mi espiritu y mente. Gracias Cristo Jesus y gracias a ustedes Dios los bendiga

Prison Evangelism, Inc.   PO Box 571977   Houston Texas 77257

I want to dig a little deeper. Please sender a free copy of "SEEKING GOD THROUGH PRAYER AND MEDITATION".

Name

Address 3010 chamberlayne ave

City, State, Zip Richmond VA 23227

Please tell us what you think of "How To Be A Child Of God". It help My Husband Get saved before he passed on to home with God. I thank you so much for this Book.

Prison Evangelism, Inc.   PO Box 571977   Houston Texas 77257

I want to dig a little deeper. Please sender a free copy of "SEEKING GOD THROUGH PRAYER AND MEDITATION".

Name

Address P.O. BOX 1150

City, State, Zip Henning, TN 38041

Please tell us what you think of "How To Be A Child Of God". I can say after read that Book I aint never serious call of God within 54 years that I am now and For the first time in my entire life I cryed and got down on my knee and said that prayer on page 14 and now I can say I'm a child of God but still I'm weak in the flesh and I still need spiritually hely to stay closer to God, here are my letter to you

son Evangelism, Inc.   PO Box 571977   Houston Texas 77257

Helping Prisoners Come to Christ

72019

🕊 I want to dig a little deeper.
Please sender a free copy of
"SEEKING GOD THROUGH
PRAYER AND MEDITATION".

Name

Address 11705 S. Alameda St.
City, State, Zip Lynwood, CA,
90262

Please tell us what you think of "How
To Be A Child Of God".
It opened my eyes & mind
It opened my heart & I
allowed/accepted god
in my life. Ive accepted
him as my father & savior
im seeking further
understanding. I want to
thank you for this book
I want to learn more.

🕊 I want to dig a little deeper.
Please sender a free copy of
"SEEKING GOD THROUGH
PRAYER AND MEDITATION".

Name

Address Location BLD D-03-D-13
City, State, Zip 100 Carman Avenue
East Meadow, NY 11554-1146

Please tell us what you think of "How
To Be A Child Of God".
I loe "How To Be A Child of
God", I used this book as a 30 day study and
as a result I gave myself
to God using the prayer on
Page 14. You helped me during
my darkest moment I am currently
an inmate (my first time) and will be
here for a long time. Please pray
for my children Alex and Roxane
Thank you God Bless you.

Suite 300 Houston Texas 77057

72019

🕊 I want to dig a little deeper.
Please sender a free copy of
"SEEKING GOD THROUGH
PRAYER AND MEDITATION".

Name

Address 8607 S.E Flowermound Rd
City, State, Zip lawton, OK 73501

Please tell us what you think of "How
To Be A Child Of God". It has really
opened my eyes and explained to
me how to be saved in terms that
I fully understand. Thank you for this
book it has changed my life. Could
you please send me the next book.
Thank you and GOD Bless You.
If it's possible could you send me
a (NLT) Bible.

Prison Evangelism, Inc.   PO Box 571977   Houston Texas 77257

72019

🕊 I want to dig a little deeper.
Please sender a free copy of
"SEEKING GOD THROUGH
PRAYER AND MEDITATION".

Name

Address TCCC 3614 Bill Price Rd.
City, State, Zip Dell Valle, Tx 78617
2016904

Please tell us what you think of "How
To Be A Child Of God". I Loved
It, It gave me great understanding of God and the Love
he has for us, and I do
beleave he gave his only
son to die for our sins.
and now I give my life
and soul to our lord and
saivor Jesus Christ with
all my heart and soul.
Thank you.

Prison Evangelism, Inc.   PO Box 571977   Houston Texas 77257

Helping Prisoners Become Evangelists

David Howell —   7/31

Hi My name is Brandon
I am from NC but I got in trouble
in GA, I am awaiting a prison sentence.
I have been Saved since I was a
child a recently rededicated my life and
surrendered the rest of my time to the
Lord. We hold a church service amongst
ourselves here in my dorm. Its amazing how
the Lord works and getting to see it
first hand. These Men are hungry for salvation
and things of the Lord. Personally in my
6 months here, the Holy Spirit has used
me to guide 13 men to Salvation. We have
over a dozen copies of "How to be a
child of God, witness edition". I have requested
2 copies of "Seeking God through prayer and Meditation".
A man left with one copy and there
is a line for the copy you just sent.
Can you please send more copies?!?! Any
other Litterature would be appreciated. I
wouldn't change a thing about the books just
wish we had More copies. Thank you so
much for everything you do. God Bless

                        Brandon ▮▮▮▮▮▮▮

                        Eph: 4:1

Helping Prisoners Become Evangelists

David Howell,   4-28-2016

    Hello Sir, my name is ▓▓▓▓▓▓▓ I am currently Incarcerated at Kilby Correctional Facility in Montgomery, Alabama. I do not mean to bother you at all. I just got through reading your book on How to be a Child of God. I really enjoyed it and have shared the lesson with the entire faith dorm. Consists of 124 men. Want to emphasize that well more than half have really let go and let God take Control of their lives. Because of God, and the Seed which I found in your lesson, I have become a Soldier in God's wonderful army.

    Well the reason for this letter, and really hate to ask, I have a King James Bible, and the lessons are NLT which I can comprehend a lot better. Wanting to know if you had a NLT study addition available. Really need a bible to help me grow in God's Word. Hope this is not asking to much. Please pray about it.

        Please write Back at this address!

72019

🕊 I want to dig a little deeper.
Please sender a free copy of
"SEEKING GOD THROUGH
PRAYER AND MEDITATION".
Name ▓▓▓▓▓▓▓
Address N.K.SP   D-I BED 112
City, State, Zip P.O BOX 5005
Delano, Ca 93216

Please tell us what you think of "How
To Be A Child Of God". _____
Book was amazing it helped
me tell my story. I was
able to open up more
and let others see and
hear my testimony. I've
shared this book with
8 other people, in which
their sharing their
testimony now.

Prison Evangelism, Inc.   PO Box 571977   Houston Texas 77257

🕊 I want to dig a little deeper.
Please sender a free copy of
"SEEKING GOD THROUGH
PRAYER AND MEDITATION".
Name ▓▓▓▓▓▓▓
Address 36714 Rd. 112
City, State, Zip VISALIA CA
                    93291

Please tell us what you think of "How
To Be A Child Of God". YOUR
BOOK HAS BEEN GREAT HELP
FOR ME. I USED TO SHARE
God's WORD WITH AND it
BROUGHT JOY TO THEIR LIFE.
WATCHING AND HEARING
SOMEONE ACCEPT CHRIST
AS THEIR lord & SAVIOR,
ENCOURAGED ME TO SHARE
God's Word.

Prison Evangelism, Inc.   PO Box 571977   Houston Texas 77257

Helping Prisoners Become Evangelists

I want to dig a little deeper.
Please send a free copy of
"SEEKING GOD THROUGH
PRAYER AND MEDITATION".

Name ████████████
Address 2041 sessions st
City, State, Zip Heyburn, ID 83336

Please tell us what you think of "How
To Be A Child Of God". I really
enjoyed this book I shared it
with my tier and led a few of
them to Christ. We also do Bible
Studies as well. Could I possibly
get both books to share with
my family at home I'd really
appreciate it God Bless You!

72019

I want to dig a little deeper.
Please sender a free copy of
"SEEKING GOD THROUGH
PRAYER AND MEDITATION".

Name ████████████
Address 904 FM 686
City, State, Zip Dayton, TX 77535

Please tell us what you think of "How
To Be A Child Of God". My fav
part is around the Back of
the book, it explains and
gives step by step. How too
help others and let the Lord
work through Me. Thanks
for this gift

Prison Evangelism, Inc.   PO Box 571977   Houston Texas 77257

72019

I want to dig a little deeper.
Please sender a free copy of
"SEEKING GOD THROUGH
PRAYER AND MEDITATION".

Name ████████████
Address 11705 S. Alameda St.
City, State, Zip Lynwood CA 90202
CRDF-2700-39 up

Please tell us what you think of "How
To Be A Child Of God". I really enjoyed
this book. I was very impressed with how
easy it was to understand the story
and the message. I just read it over
and over and this book makes it easy
for me to share the good news with
other unbelievers. I'm looking forward
to receiving Seeking God and any other
information you may have that will
help me with my spiritual walk with
my Lord and Savior. Thank You.

Prison Evangelism, Inc.   PO Box 571977   Houston Texas 77257

I want to dig a little deeper.
Please send a free copy of
"SEEKING GOD THROUGH
PRAYER AND MEDITATION".

Name ████████████
Address Fulton Reception Diagnostic Center, P.O. Box 190
City, State, Zip Fulton, MO
65251

Please tell us what you think of "How
To Be A Child Of God". This book is
truly wonderful! I have never seen a gospel
tract that so clearly and so thoroughly explained
the WHOLE gospel message. All the Bible verses
listed at the back is awesome! One doesn't even
have to have a Bible to use this. Adding an excellent
guide to sharing our faith is so great! I am
so excited about finding this book. I shared
the website with my fiancé because she wants
to share her faith with others more. God bless
you and thank you for sending these to us.

Prison Evangelism, Inc.   510 Bering Dr.   Suite 300   Houston   Texas 77057

Helping Prisoners Become Evangelists

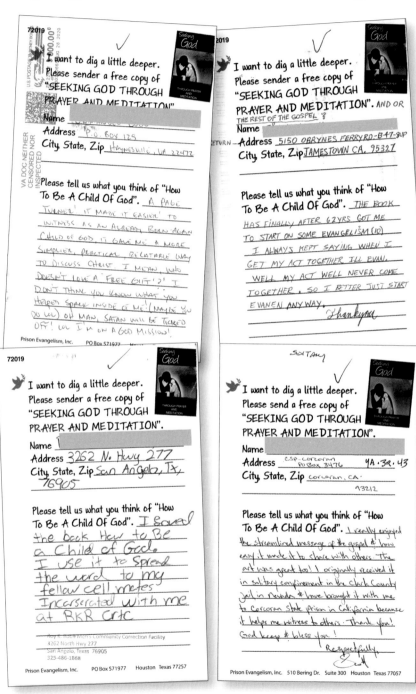

I want to dig a little deeper. Please sender a free copy of "SEEKING GOD THROUGH PRAYER AND MEDITATION"

Name ___
Address P.O. BOX 125
City, State, Zip Haynesville, VA 22472

Please tell us what you think of "How To Be A Child Of God". A PAGE TURNER! IT MADE IT EASIER TO WITNESS AS AN ALREADY BORN AGAIN CHILD OF GOD, IT GAVE ME A MORE SIMPLIER, PRACTICAL, RELATABLE WAY TO DISCUSS CHRIST. I MEAN, WHO DOESN'T LOVE A "FREE GIFT? 2"! I DON'T THINK YOU KNOW WHAT YOU HELPED SPARK INSIDE OF ME! (MAYBE YOU DO LOL) OH MAN, SATAN WILL BE TICKED OFF! LOL I'M ON A GOD MISSION!

Prison Evangelism, Inc.   PO Box 571977

I want to dig a little deeper. Please sender a free copy of "SEEKING GOD THROUGH PRAYER AND MEDITATION". AND OR THE REST OF THE GOSPEL ?

Name ___
Address 5150 OBRYNES FERRYRD-B47-8up
City, State, Zip JAMESTOWN CA. 95327

Please tell us what you think of "How To Be A Child Of God". THE BOOK HAS FINALLY AFTER 62 YRS GOT ME TO START ON SOME EVANGELISM (10) I ALWAYS KEPT SAYING WHEN I GET MY ACT TOGETHER I'LL EVAN. WELL MY ACT WELL NEVER COME TOGETHER. SO I BETTER JUST START EVANEN ANY WAY. Thank you

---

I want to dig a little deeper. Please sender a free copy of "SEEKING GOD THROUGH PRAYER AND MEDITATION".

Name ___
Address 3262 N. Hwy 277
City, State, Zip San Angelo, Tx, 76905

Please tell us what you think of "How To Be A Child Of God". I Saved the book How to Be a Child of God. I use it to spread the word to my fellow cell mates Incarcerated with me at RKR Crtc

Roy R. Robb Men's Community Correction Facility
3262 North Hwy 277
San Angelo, Texas 76905
325-486-1868

Prison Evangelism, Inc.   PO Box 571977   Houston Texas 77257

I want to dig a little deeper. Please send a free copy of "SEEKING GOD THROUGH PRAYER AND MEDITATION".

Name ___
Address CSP-Corcoran
PO Box 3476   YA·3R·43
City, State, Zip Corcoran, CA.   93212

Please tell us what you think of "How To Be A Child Of God". I really enjoyed the streamlined message of the gospel & how easy it made it to share with others. The art was great too! I originally received it in solitary confinement in the Clark County Jail in Nevada & have brought it with me to Corcoran state prison in California because it helps me witness to others. Thank you! God keep & bless you! Respectfully,

Prison Evangelism, Inc.   510 Bering Dr.   Suite 300   Houston   Texas 77057

Helping Prisoners Become Evangelists

720

🕊 I want to dig a little deeper.
Please sender a free copy of
"SEEKING GOD THROUGH
PRAYER AND MEDITATION".

Name _____
Address ▨▨ 7100 Old Alice Road
City, State, Zip ▨▨▨▨▨▨
city: Olmito, Texas ▨▨▨▨ 78575

Please tell us what you think of "How
To Be A Child Of God". It was
the perfect Book to evangalize
in prison, I know it has been
blessed and prayed over...
I used it to fish for men in
prison... During my first month
in prison about 10-12 have
accepted Jesus as their
savior and still growing
GLORY AND HONOR to the KING
OF KINGS!!! "it never RUNS out"

Prison Evangelism, Inc.   PO Box 571977   Houston Texas 77257

Thank You _____

Please Send Something to Read
to my wife who is At Home..
(address8)
Jessica _____

Prison Evangelism, Inc.
PO Box 571977
Houston, Texas 77257

720

🕊 I want to dig a little deeper.
Please sender a free copy of
"SEEKING GOD THROUGH
PRAYER AND MEDITATION".

Name _____
Address 2937 E. LAS VEGAS ST
City, State, Zip Colorado Springs
Colorado, 80906

Please tell us what you think of "How
To Be A Child Of God". IT'S BEEN
A GREAT BLESSING TO ME OVER
And over and it Helped
ME To Have The iNFo To
Lead A Friend To ChrisT.
So Keep up The Good Work
Serving Christ Jesus
Brothers And sisters

Prison Evangelism, Inc.   PO Box 571977   Houston Texas 77257

Ⓐ

🕊 I want to dig a little deeper.
Please send a free copy of
"SEEKING GOD THROUGH
PRAYER AND MEDITATION".

Name _____
Address Bizoru. Po Box 3200
City, State, Zip Goodyear, Az 85395

Please tell us what you think of "How
To Be A Child Of God". I think
it was Great the best part
are the instruction on
how to lead Others to
Christ. helping us to
help build His kingdom
and providing individuals
like myself on how to go
about doing so.

Prison Evangelism, Inc.   510 Bering Dr.   Suite 300   Houston Texas 77057

Helping To Change Families

August 10, 2016

Praise the Lord Prison Evangelism Publishers,
    My name is Oseas ███████████
currently incarcerated in McConnell Unit, Beeville
Tx. 78102.
    You recently sent a prayer book to my daughter
called, Prayer and Meditation. She has recieved
it and she is very apprecitive for your thoughts.
    I am greatly apprecitive too with you. You have
been a great blessing for my family. My daughter
just turned 17 years old now, and she told me that
she has been half way threw the book.
    Furthermore, I can say that it's hard to be
part of my familie's lives while incarcerated, but
it can be done! Thanks to ministries like yours,
we can build a bridge and a bigger relationship with
them. We grow and motivate each other emotionaly and
spiritualy together.
    I can sincerly say that it's not what you have
in your life but who you have in your life that counts.
Thank you, once again for the time and your
consideration.
                    God Bless You,
                        Sincerly, Oseas ███████

BTW: My daughters name and address is -
    Ashley ███████
    ████████████████████

Letter from Oseas, Ashley's Incarcerated Father

Helping To Change Families

Hello,

I have read the book and enjoyed it very much. I thought it was very well written and it was easy to understand. Sometimes when I'm reading the bible, I'm not sure what I'm reading about. This book broke it down for me and now I have a better understandment. But I mean, it's not like my thoughts on it matters very much, I'm just a 17 year old girl trying to strengthen my faith with God. I'm sure my dad would love the book! ~~It~~ ~~as~~ If it weren't ~~easy~~ for him, ~~so~~ ~~who other~~ who knew if I would still have faith in the Lord. Overall the book was amazing, I really hope you guys deliver it ~~to~~ those in prison so they can stay faithful, & open the eyes to nonbelievers. One question though, did my dad, Oscear ████, tell you guys to send me this book or how did you guys end up ~~to~~ finding me? ~~reading~~ ~~the book?~~

         — Ashley ████

Letter from Ashley

How God Uses the Books' Simplicity

Dear Mr. David Howell

My name is Steven M____ DC)#1,____. I read this Book How To Be A Child of God. Mr. Howell, I never read a book at one time but this book, I like it it was good real good, I want to read the next book "seeking God through Prayer and Meditation" can you plase send a free copy of it for me plase.

When, I read the Bible, I donot under stated it that good But this book had picher in it now how to be a child of the most high God we have John 3:16 tell,s me everthing, I need to know and this book showed me what are God the son of the father went and he had to do this book help me to see Clear to how to be a child of God. Now, I try hard to Call a prayer Call in prison were, I am at.

I Thank you for loving us anuff to want to know how this book can help us Thank you for Caring about God's pepok to. And Thank God for you and I pray that God Bless you and your famliys. Amen!

your new Bother in
Christ Jesus
Steven M____
TDC) #____

How God Uses the Books' Simplicity

I CAN'T READ OR WRIGHT GOOBE SO I HOPE U CAN READ THIS LOL BUT I AME LUKING AND YOUR BOOK HOW TO BE A CHILD OF GOD IS A REALL GOOBE BOOK AND IT IS EAZZEY 4 ME TO READ AND IT HELPS ME UNDERSTAND GOD BEATERY I THANK IT IS A REALLY GOOBE BOOK AND WOLBE HELP ENNY 1 UNDERSTAND GOD BEATERY AND IT IS HELPING ME IN MORE WAYS THAN 1 SO I REALLY WANT TO BI3 A LITTLE DEEPER PLEASE SEND A FREE COPY OF SEEKING GOD THROUGH PRAYER AND MEDITATION THANK YOU

JOSHUA ▮▮▮▮▮ #▮▮▮▮
EASTERN KY CORRECTIONAL COMPLEX
200 RD TO JUSTICE
WEST LIBERTY KY 41472

How God Uses the Books' Simplicity

Dear friend,

I thoroughly enjoyed the book. It was made and designed so even my grandchildren could understand it. God Bless you for the book and as I read some portions of the scriptures daily I will pass it on to other inmates who need to know Jesus. God Bless & Thank you.

Kathy

Wetumpka, Al.
36092

How God Uses the Books' Simplicity

72019

I want to dig a little deeper. Please sender a free copy of "SEEKING GOD THROUGH PRAYER AND MEDITATION".

Name ▮▮▮▮▮▮▮
Address P.O. Box 1529
City, State, Zip Corpus Christi, TX
78403

Please tell us what you think of "How To Be A Child Of God". Thank you for your booklet, I really enjoyed it. After reading it through, I went over the scripture, starting at page one, to the end of the book again, using the verses you have at the back of the book - I marked each one, as I found and read them off :) I look forward to helping to spread the word, and introducing others more to the Lord! I look forward to receiving your next book! Thanks again! Happy Holidays :) - V.C.

Prison Evangelism, Inc.   PO Box 571977   Houston Texas 77257

Ⓐ

I want to dig a little deeper. Please send a free copy of "SEEKING GOD THROUGH PRAYER AND MEDITATION".

Name ▮▮▮▮▮▮▮
Address 302 Corrections Dr
City, State, Zip Newport AR
72112

Please tell us what you think of "How To Be A Child Of God". This Book is the first Book about GOD that I truly could relate to. I loved this Book Thank you !!

▮▮▮▮▮ Dr. Suite 300   Houston Texas 77057

I want to dig a little deeper. Please send a free copy of "SEEKING GOD THROUGH PRAYER AND MEDITATION".

Name ▮▮▮▮▮▮▮
Address 2001 E. CENTRAL AVE.
City, State, Zip TOLEDO, OHIO, 43608
✶ UNITED STATES OF AMERICA ✶

Please tell us what you think of "How To Be A Child Of God". I THINK ITS VERY "HELPFUL" FOR PEOPLE "NEW" IN THE FAITH LIKE MYSELF. SOMETIMES, RELIGIOUS MATERIAL (CHRISTIAN) CAN BE LONG, DRAWN OUT & COMPLICATED WHICH MAKES GOD / JESUS "HARD TO FIND". THIS BOOK KEEPS IT SIMPLE & STRAIGHT TO THE POINT THOUGH. ANY & EVERYBODY SHOULD BE ABLE TO COMPREHEND "A CHILD OF GOD" (FROM OLD LADIES TO LIL' BABIES). GLAD I GOT AN OPPORTUNITY TO READ IT.

Prison Evangelism, Inc.   510 Bering Dr.   Suite 300   Houston Texas 77057

I want to dig a little deeper. Please send a free copy of "SEEKING GOD THROUGH PRAYER AND MEDITATION".

Name ▮▮▮▮▮▮▮
Address Algoa Correctional Center
City, State, Zip 8501 No More Victims Rd.
Jefferson City MO. 65101

Please tell us what you think of "How To Be A Child Of God". I think this is an amazing booklet. I love how powerfully simple you have made the concept of leaving our old self behind to move forward with Christ. If you have more of these, please let me know how I can obtain them. I don't have much access to things like this here. Thank you and God Bless!

Prison Evangelism, Inc.   510 Bering Dr.   Suite 300   Houston Texas 77057

How God Uses the Books' Simplicity

I want to dig a little deeper. Please send a free copy of "SEEKING GOD THROUGH PRAYER AND MEDITATION".

Name [redacted]
Address 1302 Evelyn Ave.
City, State, Zip Albany, Ga. 31705

Please tell us what you think of "How To Be A Child Of God". I really enjoyed it and it also broke down alot of things to the simplist form made it really easy to understand. The scriptures at the bottom really helped out alot as well. That small Booklet is so life changing it's Amazing!

Prison Evangelism, Inc. 510 Bering Dr. Suite 300

72019

I want to dig a little deeper. Please sender a free copy of "SEEKING GOD THROUGH PRAYER AND MEDITATION".

Name [redacted]
Address COYOTE RIDGE CORRECTIONS CENTER 1301 N. Ephrata Ave.
City, State, Zip Connell, WA 99326-0769

Please tell us what you think of "How To Be A Child Of God". As relatively new convert from Islam (3 yrs, 4 mos), I appreciate the "Child-like" simplicity of this small yet powerful book. The Holy Spirit truly is working through Prison Evangelism Inc. I can't wait to "[SEEK] GOD THROUGH PRAYER AND MEDITATION." Thank you and God Bless

Marie Roberts

Prison Evangelism, Inc. PO Box 571977 Houston Texas 77257

72019

I want to dig a little deeper. Please sender a free copy of "SEEKING GOD THROUGH PRAYER AND MEDITATION".

Name [redacted]
Address 9055 Spur 591
City, State, Zip Amarillo, Tx 79107

Please tell us what you think of "How To Be A Child Of God". I love how you simplified evangelising and salvation through Christ Jesus. I will cherish this book and share it with those I come into contacts with

Prison Evangelism, Inc. PO Box 571977 Houston Texas 77257

I want to dig a little deeper. Please sender a free copy of "SEEKING GOD THROUGH PRAYER AND MEDITATION".

Name [redacted]
Address 2605 Parker Rd
City, State, Zip Houston, Texas 77093

Please tell us what you think of "How To Be A Child Of God". I really enjoyed reading this book. I Loved how everything was broke down and very easy to understand. I appreciate easy to read books like this one. You have truly help me to open my heart and have faith in Jesus.

Prison Evangelism, Inc. PO Box 571977 Houston Texas 77257

How God Uses the Books' Illustrations

Besides
the new book
...ay I have permission to my
...o write out the prayer into my
of accepting Christ into my
...journal? And use scripture references
in my journal? Please and thank you. :)

Prison Evangeli...
PO Box 571977
Houston, Texa...

72019

I want to dig a little deeper.
Please sender a free copy of
"SEEKING GOD THROUGH
PRAYER AND MEDITATION".

Name ▮▮▮▮▮▮

Address 5150 O'Byrnes Ferry Rd.

City, State, Zip Jamestown, CA 95327

Sierra Conservation Center

Please tell us what you think of "How
To Be A Child Of God". I Loved
it. It was awesome. Yes
I accept Jesus to live through
me. It made so much sense,
with the pictures. My favorite
is Christ on the cross
bridging the gap and the Lord
lifting us up. Also with God
inside us. Pg. 22 and 36. Thank
you. God bless you.
          I have a request

Prison Evangelism, Inc.   PO Box 571977   Houston Texas 77257

72019

I want to dig a little deeper.
Please sender a free copy of
"SEEKING GOD THROUGH
PRA▮▮▮

Name Dustin Tatum #613839

Address 960 State Route 212

City, State, Zip Tiptonville TN 38079-4037

Please tell us what you think of "How
To Be A Child Of God". I Love
this colorful comic style book
Witness Edition of "How to be
A Child of God". This percet
quality paperback is so fun to read
all the bright colors and illustrations
in this "Comic style" edition taught
me alot about being a child of
God. It kept my attention and was
So fun to read. I can't wait to
recieve the "Seeking God through Prayer &
Meditation" Edition.

Prison Evangelism, Inc.   PO Box 571977   Houston Texas 77257

72019

I want to dig a little deeper.
Please sender a free copy of
"SEEKING GOD THROUGH
PRAYER AND MEDITATION".

Name ▮▮▮▮▮▮

Address 101 E. Methvin

City, State, Zip Longview TX 75601

Please tell us what you think of "How
To Be A Child Of God". I
absolutely loved the
book and the pictures!
I littrally cried
when saying the
prayer!

Prison Evangelism, Inc.   PO Box 571977   Houston Texas 77257

How God Uses the Books' Illustrations

72019

I want to dig a little deeper. Please sender a free copy of "SEEKING GOD THROUGH PRAYER AND MEDITATION".

Name _____
Address N.K.S.P. FACILITY D2 #133 P.O. Box 5005
City, State, Zip DELANO, CA 93216

Please tell us what you think of "How To Be A Child Of God". I LOVED THE EASY TO UNDERSTAND COMIC DEPICTION OF THE MESSAGE/STORY! IT WAS A JOY TO READ/LOOK AT IT! VERY IMPRESSED AND I PASSED IT ALONG TO OTHER INMATES WHO ALSO ENJOYED IT AND LEARNED FROM IT.

Prison Evangelism, Inc.   PO Box 571977   Houston T...

019

I want to dig a little deeper. Please sender a free copy of "SEEKING GOD THROUGH PRAYER AND MEDITATION".

Name _____
Address 100 N Lamar
City, State, Zip Ft.Worth, Texas 76196

Please tell us what you think of "How To Be A Child Of God". I loved the book and how it explains how to witness & share the good news & the illustrations are so brilliant as well as captivating! Thank you! I can't wait for the next book!!

Houston Texas 77257

72019

I want to dig a little deeper. Please sender a free copy of "SEEKING GOD THROUGH PRAYER AND MEDITATION".

Name _____
Address 14510 Cardinal Creek Ct.
City, State, Zip Houston, Tx 77062

Please tell us what you think of "How To Be A Child Of God". Loved it, especially the illustrations. The scriptures at the back were very helpful in showing where in the bible each pages scriptures that are also listed at the bottom of each page.

Prison Evangelism, Inc.   PO Box 571977   Houston Texas 77257

72019

I want to dig a little deeper!! Please sender a free copy of "SEEKING GOD THROUGH PRAYER AND MEDITATION".

Name _____
Address 7320 New Kent Highway
City, State, Zip Barhamsville, Virginia 23011

Please tell us what you think of "How To Be A Child Of God". I loved it! The illustrations were perfect! The story is perfect, it will touched my heart and soul! I have the prayer (pg. 14) posted up on my wall! I have taped 2 other pages on my folder that I use daily to remind me of How Much God Loves me & my husband & daughter. Thank you! Hope to hear back soon.

Prison Evangelism, Inc.   PO Box 571977   Houston Texas 77257

How God Uses the Books' Illustrations

Card 1 (019):

🕊 I want to dig a little deeper. Please send a free copy of "SEEKING GOD THROUGH PRAYER AND MEDITATION".

Name ▓▓▓▓▓▓▓▓

Address 3337 Hwy 44

City, State, Zip Owensboro, KY 48303

Please tell us what you think of "How To Be A Child Of God". I love the way it presents the gospel. A friend of mine who can't read saw the pictures and asked me to read it to them. So it was an excellent attention grabber.

Card 2:

🕊 I want to dig a little deeper. Please sender a free copy of "SEEKING GOD THROUGH PRAYER AND MEDITATION".

Name ▓▓▓▓▓▓▓▓

Address 20710 LEAPWOOD AVE.

City, State, Zip Carson, CA 90746 SUITE D.

Please tell us what you think of "How To Be A Child Of God". WOW! I've never seen a book or even read one like this! The pictures are what brings all the words to life! GODS MESSAGE comes across soo much clearer this way! I absolutely loved this read.

Card 3 (720):

🕊 I want to dig a little deeper. Please sender a free copy of "SEEKING GOD THROUGH PRAYER AND MEDITATION".

Name ▓▓▓▓▓▓▓▓

Address P.O. Box 1010

City, State, Zip Canon City, CO 81215 CDC / CH3 / B2N2 / CTCF

Please tell us what you think of "How To Be A Child Of God". Thank you for this book. I have read it numerous times. On 31 August is when I gave myself to the Lord. I am a born again Christian and I loved the illustration as well as the words. The word speaks to you but the artwork spoke more to me. Amazing!!!

Prison Evangelism, Inc.   PO Box 571977   Houston Texas 77257

Card 4 (72019):

🕊 I want to dig a little deeper. Please sender a free copy of "SEEKING GOD THROUGH PRAYER AND MEDITATION".

Name ▓▓▓▓▓▓▓▓

Address Hampton Roads Regional Jail

City, State, Zip Portsmouth, VA 23707 P.O. Box 7609

Please tell us what you think of "How To Be A Child Of God". Awesome! I think everyone need a copy just send it to every address.... This book helps with the visual and give us a taste of what walking with Christ look & feel like. Teenagers come to mind on who this book can really help and young adults.... everyone. Thank You. Personal Testimony just amazing! I passed my copy to a young man and he gave his life to Christ and saved his relationship at home.

Prison Evangelism, Inc.   PO Box 571977   Houston Texas 77257

How God Uses the Books' Illustrations

72019

I want to dig a little deeper. Please sender a free copy of "SEEKING GOD THROUGH PRAYER AND MEDITATION".

Name ▮▮▮▮▮▮▮▮▮▮

Address 503 E EDMONOS

City, State, Zip SAN ANTONIO TX 78214

Please tell us what you think of "How To Be A Child Of God". AWESOM I WILL BE USING IT TO REACH OTHERS WHO KNOW WHO I HUNG WITH BEFORE I CAME TO PRISON 2½ YEARS AGO I WILL BE GOING HOME 9/28/19 TO BRING THEM OUT OF THE DARK WORLD INTO THE LIGHT OF OUR SAVIOUR WHO PROTECT SUSTAIN AND GUIDE US. THANK YOU SO MUCH, I WAS LOST BLIND BUT I'm FOUND AND NOW I SEE THANK YOU JESUS.

Prison Evangelism, Inc. ▮▮▮

I want to dig a little deeper. Please sender a free copy of "SEEKING GOD THROUGH PRAYER AND MEDITATION".

Name Rachel Walker

Address P.O. Box 509

City, State, Zip Mason, TN 38049

Please tell us what you think of "How To Be A Child Of God". This book has been helpful for me and the other women here that I've shared it with, both those of us who were familiar with God and those of us who were new. I love how the content is simple, streamlined, visual, and true with scriptural references. Thank you for offering these books, now I'm an excited witness for Christ!

I want to dig a little deeper. Please send a free copy of "SEEKING GOD THROUGH PRAYER AND MEDITATION".

Name ▮▮▮▮▮▮▮▮▮▮

Address FT DIX FCI P.O. BOX 2000

City, State, Zip JOINT BASE MDL, NJ 08640

Please tell us what you think of "How To Be A Child Of God". I'M A PASTOR, INCARCERATED FOR TAX VIOLATIONS BUT WORKING TO LEAD MEN TO JESUS. I HOLD BIBLE STUDIES / PRAYER TIME FOR MEN HERE SEEKING THE LORD. I DISTRIBUTED SEVERAL OF "HOW TO BE A CHILD OF GOD" IF YOU CAN SEND 10 OF THE "SEEKING GOD..." BOOKS I'LL MAKE SURE THEY GET INTO THE HANDS OF MEN HERE.

Prison Evangelism, Inc. 510 Bering Dr. Suite 300 Houston Texas 77057

I want to dig a little deeper. Please send a free copy of "SEEKING GOD THROUGH PRAYER AND MEDITATION".

Name ▮▮▮▮▮▮▮▮▮▮

Address P.O Box 709

City, State, Zip Alto Ga 30510

Please tell us what you think of "How To Be A Child Of God". I absolutely loved it! I was in county jail when I got it and it inspired me to start a bible study group!! It was a wonderful inspiration I'm so glad I have a chance for this issue!

Prison Evangelism, Inc. 510 Bering Dr. Suite 300 Houston Texas 77057

How the Books' are Used for Ministry

I want to dig a little deeper. ✓
Please send a free copy of
"SEEKING GOD THROUGH
PRAYER AND MEDITATION".

Name ▮

Address MSP Unit 29 F B-128

City, State, Zip Parchman MS
38738

Please tell us what you think of "How
To Be A Child Of God". This is the most
theologically sound, compact summary of
the message of the Bible/Gospel I have
ever seen.   I have passed out, and
used in ministry, "How to Be A Child of God"
more than any other material I possess.
     I am an IRA (Inmate Religious Assistant)
at Parchman — a graduate of NOBTS (Parchman
Ext).   Is there any way I can recieve
more of these books as well as Seeking God,
that I may use/distribute?

Prison Evangelism, Inc. 510 Bering Dr. Suite 300 Hous...

72019

I want to dig a little deeper. ✓
Please sender a free copy of
"SEEKING GOD THROUGH
PRAYER AND MEDITATION".

Name Eric Fort Worth

Address PO Box 15330

City, State, Zip Fort Worth, TX 76119

Please tell us what you think of "How
To Be A Child Of God". We did it
as a group study (About 15 of us) and
we really enjoyed it, and got a lot
out of it. We are hoping to be able
to do the same thing with "Seeking God
Through Prayer + Meditation".

Thank you so much for all that you
do in the name of Christ !!!

I want to dig a little deeper. ✓
Please send a free copy of
"SEEKING GOD THROUGH
PRAYER AND MEDITATION".

Name ▮

Address Plane State Unit 904 FM 686

City, State, Zip Dayton, TX 77535

Please tell us what you think of "How
To Be A Child Of God". Amazing!
It was direct + easy to Read +
understand for everyone - no matter
how far along their walk they are!
I minister to alot of women in my
dorm here in prison- great tool!
Please send any + all books +
materials you have available to
show Christ's love in this very dark
place! God Bless you! - Danielle

Prison Evangelism, Inc. 510 Bering Dr. Suite 300 Houston Texas 77057

I want to dig a little deeper. ✓
Please send a free copy of
"SEEKING GOD THROUGH
PRAYER AND MEDITATION".

Name ▮

Address 221 North Timber st.

City, State, Zip Brandon MS 39042

Please tell us what you think of "How
To Be A Child Of God". I think
it was a true Blessing from
God, I do BIBLE STUDY with
alot of inmates in the jail
and it has helped me bring
others to Church with God
and save them too. Thank
you so very much! I'm a
BLUE SUIT Trustie here and I'm
all about learning and giving more
of Jesus... Please send more

Prison Evangelism, Inc. 510 Bering Dr. Suite 300 Houston Texas 77057

How the Books' are Used for Ministry

72019

☑ ✈ I want to dig a little deeper.
Please sender a free copy of
"SEEKING GOD THROUGH
PRAYER AND MEDITATION".

Name ▮▮▮▮▮▮
Address 503 E EDMONDS
City, State, Zip SAN ANTONIO TX
78214

Please tell us what you think of "How
To Be A Child Of God". AWESOM
I WILL BE USING IT TO
REACH OTHERS WHO KNOW WHO
I HUNG WITH BEFORE I CAME
TO PRISON 2 1/2 YEARS AGO I WILL
BE GOING HOME 9/28/19 TO BRING
THEM OUT OF THE DARK WORLD
INTO THE LIGHT OF OUR SAVIOUR
WHO PROTECT SUSTAIN AND GUIDE US.
THANK YOU SO MUCH, I WAS LOST BLIND
BUT I'm FOUND AND NOW I SEE THANK YOU
JESUS.
FOR THIS TIME
Prison Evangelism, Inc.   PO Box 571977   Houston Texas 77257 IN HERE
THIS IS WHAT IT

72019

☑ ✈ I want to dig a little deeper.
Please sender a free copy of
"SEEKING GOD THROUGH
PRAYER AND MEDITATION".

Name ▮▮▮▮▮▮
Address P.O. Box 509
City, State, Zip Mason, TN 38049

Please tell us what you think of "How
To Be A Child Of God". This book
has been helpful for me and the other
women here that I've shared it with, both
those of us who were familiar with God and
those of us who were new. I love how the
content is simple, streamlined, visual, and
true with scriptural references. Thank you for
offering these books, now I'm an excited
witness for Christ!

Prison Evangelism, Inc.   PO Box 571977   Houston Texas 77257

Lord 10/8y

☑ ✈ I want to dig a little deeper.
Please send a free copy of
"SEEKING GOD THROUGH
PRAYER AND MEDITATION".

Name ▮▮▮▮▮▮
Address FT DIX FCI
P.O. BOX 2000
City, State, Zip JOINT BASE MDL,
NJ 08640

Please tell us what you think of "How
To Be A Child Of God". I'M A
PASTOR, INCARCERATED FOR TAX VIOLATIONS
BUT WORKING TO LEAD MEN TO JESUS.
I HOLD BIBLE STUDIES / PRAYER TIME
FOR MEN HERE SEEKING THE LORD.
I DISTRIBUTED SEVERAL OF "HOW TO
BE A CHILD OF GOD" IF YOU CAN
SEND 10 OF THE "SEEKING GOD …"
BOOKS I'LL MAKE SURE THEY GET
INTO THE HANDS OF MEN HERE.

Prison Evangelism, Inc.   510 Bering Dr.   Suite 300   Houston Texas 77057

☑ ✈ I want to dig a little deeper.
Please send a free copy of
"SEEKING GOD THROUGH
PRAYER AND MEDITATION".

Name ▮▮▮▮▮▮
Address P.O. Box 709
City, State, Zip Alto Ga
30510

Please tell us what you think of "How
To Be A Child Of God". I
absolutely loved it!
I was in county jail
when I got it and
it inspired me to
start a bible study
group!! It was a
wonderful inspiration
I'm so glad I have
a chance for this
issue!

Prison Evangelism, Inc.   510 Bering Dr.   Suite 300   Houston Texas 77057

"I Love This Book"

10-3-20

May I tell you how happy to be writing you with The Love of GOD! Everything that you and the evangelism has been a blessing for us here. There is a couple of men here that wanted me to write you this letter to ask if you have any Books in Spanish:

How to Be A Child of GOD?

By David Howell.

We pray that you receive this letter in good health and with the Love of GOD, Please write Back and let us know.

"I Love This Book"

72019

🕊 I want to dig a little deeper.
Please send a free copy of
"SEEKING GOD THROUGH
PRAYER AND MEDITATION".
Name _____
Address L.C.C. 15976 Hwy 165
City, State, Zip O11A , LA 71465

Please tell us what you think of "How
To Be A Child Of God". MOST
Amazing Thing
That ever Happend
in my whole Life

Prison Evangelism, Inc.   510 Bering Dr.   Suite 300   Houston Texas 77057

72019

🕊 I want to dig a little deeper.
Please sender a free copy of
"SEEKING GOD THROUGH
PRAYER AND MEDITATION".

Name _____
Address 1210 Coryell City Rd.
City, State, Zip Gatesville, TX 76528

Please tell us what you think of "How
To Be A Child Of God". _____
It was very comforting to
me and I read it daily,
the scriptures in the back.
I have no Bible, but I
treasure this booklet. Its
all I have to read to
find comfort and peace.

Prison Evangelism, Inc.   PO Box 571977   Houston Texas 77257

72019

🕊 I want to dig a little deeper.
Please sender a free copy of
"SEEKING GOD THROUGH
PRAYER AND MEDITATION".

Name _____
Address 742. Fm. 712
City, State, Zip Marlin, Tx. 76661

Please tell us what you think of "How
To Be A Child Of God". Smile !!!
Honestly, I cryed while
I read Because it deeply
touched my heart in more
ways than one, towards
the Blessed Point where I
sincerely want to know and
learn more about God. I
whole-heartedly Think the
"How to Be a Child of God"
Book's a very best that
Ive ever read my whole life!
Prison Evangelism, Inc.   PO Box 571977   Houston Texas 77257
★ PLEASE SEND me the NEXT one! thanks!

72019

🕊 I want to dig a little deeper.
Please sender a free copy of
"SEEKING GOD THROUGH
PRAYER AND MEDITATION".
Name _____
Address 4430 Calle Real Rd.
City, State, Zip Santa Barbara,
CA 93110

Please tell us what you think of "How
To Be A Child Of God". I loved
the message &
I was in a bad
place when I read it a
I instally felt loved,
I felt like I got this
book for a reason.
I'm thankful for the
book & I would like to
get to know more.
Prison Evangelism, Inc.   PO Box 571977   Houston Texas 77257

"I Love This Book"

Card 1 (72019):

I want to dig a little deeper. Please sender a free copy of "SEEKING GOD THROUGH PRAYER AND MEDITATION".

Name ▓▓▓▓▓
Address 3800 Fountain Ainne
City, State, Zip Atmore AL 36503

Please tell us what you think of "How To Be A Child Of God". I love This Book it change The out Look of my life now I see God as he really is it help me to understand my heavenly Father mor better

Card 2 (72019):

I want to dig a little deeper. Please sender a free copy of "SEEKING GOD THROUGH PRAYER AND MEDITATION".

Name ▓▓▓▓▓
Address P.O. Box 239
City, State, Zip la Villa, TX, 78562

Please tell us what you think of "How To Be A Child Of God". I asked GOD to bless me with a daily Meditation book this book is perfect because I also been wanting a comic book. He sure knows our hearts desires. Please pray for me

Card 3 (72019):

I want to dig a little deeper. Please sender a free copy of "SEEKING GOD THROUGH PRAYER AND MEDITATION".

Name ▓▓▓▓▓
Address Wilme Unit 810 FM 2821
City, State, Zip Huntsville TX 77349

Please tell us what you think of "How To Be A Child Of God". It was very educational I like the way thy all put it on some street type of stuff Please send any information you have on that type of stuff. I'm very curios. I'm a muslim that reads the Bible every day but Seeking God got my attention 4-real. Thank You Robert Levy

Prison Evangelism, Inc. PO Box 571977 Houston Texas 77257

Card 4:

I want to dig a little deeper. Please send a free copy of "SEEKING GOD THROUGH PRAYER AND MEDITATION".

Name ▓▓▓▓▓ 6C
Address S.S.C.F. 4295 R.T. 47
City, State, Zip Delmont, New Jersey 08314

Please tell us what you think of "How To Be A Child Of God". It Was the Best Book I Ever Read in my Life. I fell in Love with it Thank you So much.

Prison Evangelism, Inc. 510 Bering Dr. Suite 300 Houston Texas 77057

"I Love This Book"

I want to dig a little deeper.
Please send a free copy of
"SEEKING GOD THROUGH
PRAYER AND MEDITATION".
Name
Address S.S.C.F. 4295 R.T.47
City, State, Zip Delmont,
New Jersey 08314

Please tell us what you think of "How
To Be A Child Of God". It
Was the Best Book I
Ever Read in my
Life I fell in Love
With it Thank you
So much.

Prison Evangelism, Inc. 510 Bering Dr. Suite 300 Houston Texas 77057

72019

I want to dig a little deeper.
Please sender a free copy of
"SEEKING GOD THROUGH
PRAYER AND MEDITATION".
Name
Address ROBERTSON UNIT, 12071 F.M. 3522
City, State, Zip ABILENE, TEXAS 79601-8799

Please tell us what you think of "How
To Be A Child Of God". I found it to
be revealing and resourceful in bringing myself
and others into the understanding of what it means
to have CHRIST. Especially for those who
mistaken, feel that we're saved on account
of the good deeds we do. When in fact its
only through our FAITH and belief in
CHRIST That we're saved! I've shared this
news and book with people who are willing
to accept it. And it made me want to learn more.

Prison Evangelism, Inc. PO Box 571977 Houston Texas 77257

I want to dig a little deeper.
Please send a free copy of
"SEEKING GOD THROUGH
PRAYER AND MEDITATION".
Name B
Address P.O. BOX 2000
City, State, Zip LAWTEY, Florida 32058
"LAWTEY CORRECTIONAL INSTITUTION"

Please tell us what you think of "How
To Be A Child Of God". I Really Loved
Your Book "How To Be a Child of God"!
AT FIRST I Thought it Would be Silly.
But once I STARTED Reading it The
Book Was Sooo Good, I couldn't Put
it Down. It Was Like God Speaking,
RIGHT THROUGH The Book (To JUST ME).
I MAZINE how That Book IMPACTED My
Life. One Word to DeCRIbe it —
"AWESOME"!!! Thank you
Sincerely

Prison Evangelism, Inc. 510 Bering Dr. Suite 300 Houston Texas 77057

I want to dig a little deeper.
Please sender a free copy of
"SEEKING GOD THROUGH
PRAYER AND MEDITATION".
Name
Address B2A #208
City, State, Zip P.O. box 5500
WASCO CA, 93280

Please tell us what you think of "How
To Be A Child Of God". I really
enjoyed "How To be A child of god"
I had found it on a book cart here
in Prison. It was verry fulfilling
and inlighting and I had passed
it around for other enmates to read
aswell. Thank you for offing us
inmates an oppertunity to gain
Knowledge of christ's sacrifices
and an easyer reading style.
God bless.

Prison Evangelism, Inc. PO Box 571977 Houston Texas 77257

"I Love This Book"

Card A (top left):

No friends or family, just+ beginning

I want to dig a little deeper.
Please send a free copy of
"SEEKING GOD THROUGH
PRAYER AND MEDITATION".

Name
Address 1800 Luther Drive
City, State, Zip NAVASOTA, TX 77868

Please tell us what you think of "How
To Be A Child Of God". IM JUST
LUNINY I 38 & WANT TO
LURN mor im DISLEXiK But
I Do TriY hard TO feeD The
BiBle your Books Are So AllSun
for me I have now Frends
or FAMLY im iN PriZiN & GOD
& Jesus is All iHAVE I HAVE NO
one els ID Love iNY & evirYthing
you CAN SiND me PLees &
god BLESS YOU ALL Ther!

Prison Evangelism, Inc. 510 Bering Dr. Suite 300 Houston Texas 77057

Card A (top right):

I want to dig a little deeper.
Please send a free copy of
"SEEKING GOD THROUGH
PRAYER AND MEDITATION".

Name
Address 12120 Savage Dr.
City, State, Zip MIdway, Texas 75852

Please tell us what you think of "How
To Be A Child Of God". I think Personally
it is A good understanding for A Person seeking
god All the Person has to do is Believe And trust
in him with your heart And he will work
miracles I love the Bible verses in the back
of the book it enlighten me on some instruction
im 21 years old And I'm learning as I go Alot And
Faster than others not to brag But I take the
little things As Blessing too I Pray every day And
ask for things And I can see myself changing Fast

Prison Evangelism, Inc. 510 Bering Dr. Suite 300 Houston Texas 77057

Card (bottom left):

I want to dig a little deeper.
Please send a free copy of
"SEEKING GOD THROUGH
PRAYER AND MEDITATION".

Name
Address 12120 Savage dr
City, State, Zip Midway, TX.
75852

Please tell us what you think of "How
To Be A Child Of God". It
touched me, I am new
to the bible and want
to learn the word of it.
Please Send some Bible
studys if you can
Please, Thank you

Prison Evangelism, Inc. 510 Bering Dr. Suite 300 Houston Texas 77057

Card (bottom right):

"SEEKING GOD THROUGH
PRAYER AND MEDITATION".

Name
Address Boulder county jail 3200 Air Port Road
City, State, Zip Boulder, CO. 80301

Please tell us what you think of "How
To Be A Child Of God". The Lord our Savior
Told me to pick This Book up.
I Praised Him for it.
you Told The Truth in The Book.
I like The ART work.
I always be a child of God, keep praying.

UNCENSORED
INMATE MAIL
BOULDER COUNTY JAIL

Prison Evangelism, Inc. 510 Bering Dr. Suite 300 Houston Texas 77057

Helping Prisoners Grow Spiritually

Nov. 17th, 2019

Dear Prison Evangelism,

Seeking God through Prayer and Meditation was even better than 'A Child of God'. It was extremely enlightening. My favorite part was learning how to pray using ACTS. Also the 21 days of prayer I am now doing. I love how you refer back with the Bible verses to which they apply with each lesson. I've learned a lot about prayer and meditation and my relationship with God is stronger because of BOTH your books. I've passed along both books to my fellow inmates. Don't change a thing! BOOK was Fantastic. I am truly blessed to have recieved it. Anything else you have I would love to read and PASS along.

Sincerely,

Kacy,

Helping Prisoners Grow Spiritually

Card 1 (top left)

72019

✓

I want to dig a little deeper. Please sender a free copy of "SEEKING GOD THROUGH PRAYER AND MEDITATION".

Name ▓▓▓▓▓▓▓ #

Address 5030 Jefferson County Jail

City, State, Zip Beaumont, TX 77705 Hwy 69 S

Please tell us what you think of "How To Be A Child Of God".
I loved it! I'VE BEEN TRYING REAL HARD TO GET TO KNOW OUR GOD. AND IT JUST OPEN MY EYES EVEN MORE ABOUT HIM.
THANK YOU!

Card 2 (top right)

✓

I want to dig a little deeper. Please send a free copy of "SEEKING GOD THROUGH PRAYER AND MEDITATION".

Name ▓▓▓▓▓▓▓

Address Lovelock Correctional Center, 1200 Prison Rd

City, State, Zip Lovelock, Nevada 89419

Please tell us what you think of "How To Be A Child Of God". I really enjoyed it. It really went in depth and explained things I didn't quite understand before. Reading this book helped me through a very dark time in my life and gave me hope. Since reading it my relationship with God has grown.

Prison Evangelism, Inc.   510 Bering Dr.   Suite 300   Houston   Texas 77057

Card 3 (bottom left)

✓ sent 6/27/18

yes

I want to dig a little deeper. Please send a free copy of "SEEKING GOD THROUGH PRAYER AND MEDITATION".

Name ▓▓▓

Address 1245 Camp Rd.

City, State, Zip SALISBURY NC. 28147

Please tell us what you think of "How To Be A Child Of God". It's good to know that I can Love Like GOD AND Be a Light for Him to help other See Him to. AND that I'm A man of GOD!!

Prison Evangelism, Inc.   510 Bering Dr.   Suite 300   Houston   Texas 77057

Card 4 (bottom right)

✓ sent 6/27/18

yes

I want to dig a little deeper. Please send a free copy of "SEEKING GOD THROUGH PRAYER AND MEDITATION".

Name ▓▓▓▓▓▓▓

Address 1245 Camp Rd.

City, State, Zip SALISBURY NC. 28147

Please tell us what you think of "How To Be A Child Of God". It's good to know that I can Love Like GOD AND Be a Light for Him to help other See Him to. AND that I'm A man of GOD!!

Prison Evangelism, Inc.   510 Bering Dr.   Suite 300   Houston   Texas 77057

Helping Prisoners Grow Spiritually

Prison Evangelism Publishers,   3-2-20

    Your books How to be a child of God and Seeking God through Prayer and Meditation are really really Great books. As a beginner in the Christain world these books are a great start and guide. Thank you Prison Evangelism Publishers for these books for changing my life and making it easer on me to under God and prayer plus meditation. God Bless you all and again thank you

Jamarr

PS: Keep up the good work

Helping Prisoners Grow Spiritually

To: The publishers of Seeking God through prayer & meditation

    I am really getting alot out of this book. Being in prison leaves a person with time to think or meditate rather. Now whether they meditate on worrisome things that cause more anxiety or God's word and their past choices and future better choices is up to them. This book can help guide your thoughts towards a more positive thought process and meditation if a person will use the helpful advice given. Also I like how it follows along with things you learn in the 12 steps and really breaks the step down alot more. Such as taking a personal inventory of our wrongs or "Sin life Inventory" and asking God to remove these defects of Character. This is something I have found is good to do every so often. Write them down then pray about it. I hope you will be publishing more books like this soon. Or if you have any others already published please send them to me if possible. Please & Thank you

Shantaye
ACC # 75

Helping Prisoners Grow Spiritually

good morning

From: Djibril, S ████████
████████

I Really thank u For the Book u Send me
that help me get closer and closer to
god. I learn to Be thankfull what
god ~~dead~~ has Sent in my life.

This Book Showed me the true meaning of
Christian meditation and Seeking and
Asking god For Forgivness and change.
In my Life. And Showed me to.
Guard my HEART. And to Be Always
Thankfull. And Thinking AHEAD AND
Resetting your mind. AND TO BE REAL
And Acceptance me Surrender. And
A change of Personality. And Pray

through Jesus. and Let Jesus Show
through you. And Jesus Living his
Life Through us. That's Real I
change my Life. I'm A single man
Now. Send me A <u>Bible</u> Thank
you P.S

Helping Prisoners Grow Spiritually

Tuesday 9, 2020

Dear Prison Evangelism, Inc
Brother David Howell.

I'm just writing To let you know That I am enjoying
The New book- Seeking God Through PRAYER and
meditation, I would not Change Nothing. It is giving
me alot of answers That I Needed. Especially
in PRAying, I am a siNNER, and It has been so
hard for me To ask For forgiveness, I sometime
Think That God does not want To forgive me
I've done so many bad things To my family and
other people. This book is helping me To Think it
over, God Does Love me. I know my faith will grow
more by Reading The BIBLE and This Book you send me.
I'm a slow Reader, Because, I sometimes don't understand The Scriptures, So I have To Read Them over and
over, allso I don't have a good Education. But This
doesn't stop me From TRying- I Love God and what he's
done for me, So I just want To Thank you so much
for This book. I just started But I Know That it's
going To help me Thru some sorrows I'm going Thru.
Thank you very much

your New Friend
and brother

72019

I want to dig a little deeper.
Please sender a free copy of
"SEEKING GOD THROUGH
PRAYER AND MEDITATION".
Name ▓▓▓▓
Address PO Box 3850
City, State, Zip Adelanto
CA 92301

Please tell us what you think of "How
To Be A Child Of God". this
book open my eyes to tell
my family and friend about
God how he die for us and
"my old self has been crucified
with christ. it is no longer I
who live but christ live in me"
Galations 2.20 thank you for
this book keep giving Gods
work God bless all you!

Prison Evangelism, Inc.   PO Box 571977   Houston Texas ▓▓▓

I want to dig a little deeper.
Please sender a free copy of
"SEEKING GOD THROUGH
PRAYER AND MEDITATION".

Name ▓▓▓▓
Address 1401 State School Rd.
City, State, Zip Gatesville, Tx 76599
Gatesville Unit/Hackberry

Please tell us what you think of "How
To Be A Child Of God". I learned
how to walk with Jesus
living in me. I also feel
when I read it over and over,
that I want to earn his
honor, instead of trying
to make him notice me.

GENERAL INMATE
CORRESPONDENCE TEXAS
DEPARTMENT OF CRIMINAL
JUSTICE   CORRECTIONAL
INSTITUTIONS DIVISION

Prison Evangelism, Inc.   PO Box 571977   Houston Texas 77257

I want to dig a little deeper.
Please send a free copy of
"SEEKING GOD THROUGH
PRAYER AND MEDITATION".
Name ▓▓▓▓
Address PO Box 3673
City, State, Zip Holiday, FL
34692

Please tell us what you think of "How
To Be A Child Of God". I enjoyed
reading it + viewing the
illustrations. I like the large
print since I'm disabled and
don't see very well. The
picture on page 18 really
clarified the "In Christ"
and "Christ in me" phrases
which were a little ambiguous
before I read the book. Thank you.

Prison Evangelism, Inc.   510 Bering Dr.   Suite 300   Houston Texas 77057

I want to dig a little deeper.
Please sender a free copy of
"SEEKING GOD THROUGH
PRAYER AND MEDITATION".
Name ▓▓▓▓
Address 2809 Airport Rd - PA207A
City, State, Zip Greenwood SC
29649 - LEATH Correctional Inst.

Please tell us what you think of "How
To Be A Child Of God". ♥ ✝
I Absolutely loved it! Because
I Recently was born again.
Also, I Recently got healed
On August 19, 2019 @ 8:30 A.M.
I Am a Renewed Creation! I
turned from my old ways &
now Christ lives in me. And
Now I am so hungry for God's
WORD. Headed toward "Victory" ☺

Prison Evangelism, Inc.   PO Box 571977   Houston Texas 77257

Helping Prisoners Rely on Christ in Them

A

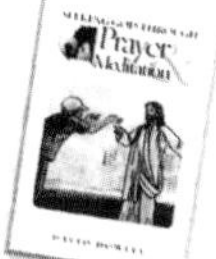

I want to dig a little deeper.
Please send a free copy of
"SEEKING GOD THROUGH
PRAYER AND MEDITATION".

Name [redacted]
Address 201 S. 4Th Ave
City, State, Zip Phoenix, ARizona
85003

Please tell us what you think of "How To Be A Child Of God". It is a Beautiful & Eye opening Story. Help'd me Straingthen the vertious that I was weak in. Tought me new prayers and made me realize that my old self is dead and my new life is alive with Christ Jesus. He in me I in him. Please Keep my family & I in Prayers, my Fiancee Brittany DelRosario may the lord our God help Her through Her Journey in Rehab. & may we Both Come out of this, Stronger in Faith with Jesus Christ!. I'm incarcerated right now & need the prayers of all my Brothers & sisters in Faith. I Know God is with me & never leaves us a lone, But if "He" our Fathers heres prayers From all His children to help their Brother his, Son, he will grant us what we ask for. Thank-u. & God Bless. I would like any literature you can Help me with to help myself. Once again God Bless ...

Prison Evangelism, Inc. 510...

Ⓐ

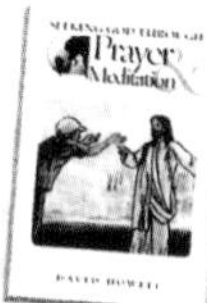

I want to dig a little deeper.
Please send a free copy of
"SEEKING GOD THROUGH
PRAYER AND MEDITATION".

Name [redacted]
Address 6564 STATE HWY 96 "3-C-5332"
City, State, Zip OLNEY SPRINGS, Colo. -81062

Please tell us what you think of "How To Be A Child Of God". I REALLY LIKED HOW IT EXPLAINED ABOUT THE LOAD WE CARRY AROUND, ALL WE HAVE TO DO IS DROP IT OFF AND JESUS WILL TAKE CARE OF IT, ALSO ONCE WE HAVE THE HOLY SPIRIT IN US WE CAN NOW SEE IT WHEN WE LOOK IN THE MIRROR

Good for understanding Christ in us

Ⓐ

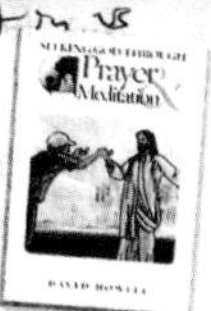

I want to dig a little deeper.
Please send a free copy of
"SEEKING GOD THROUGH
PRAYER AND MEDITATION".

Name [redacted]
Address 21 FM 247
City, State, Zip Huntsville, TX 77320

Please tell us what you think of "How To Be A Child Of God". WAS very informative. Excellent artwork and presentation of the Gospel and how to be transformed into a child of God and allow Jesus Christ to live inside & throughout us. Upon my release I plan to study it with my children and others!

Prison Evangelism, Inc. 510 Bering Dr. Suite 300 Houston Texas 77057

Ⓐ Good for telling story to young believers

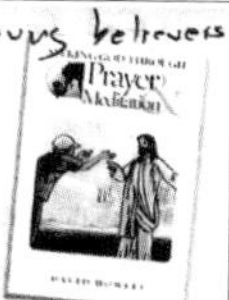

I want to dig a little deeper.
Please send a free copy of
"SEEKING GOD THROUGH
PRAYER AND MEDITATION".

Name [redacted]
Address 21 FM 247
City, State, Zip HUNTSVILLE TX 77320

Please tell us what you think of "How To Be A Child Of God". I LIKED IT ALOT. I Esp Liked All THE SCRIPTURES BACKING YOUR STORY FOR YOUNG BELIEVERS WHO DON'T KNOW THE "TRUTH" THAT WELL. I WISH MORE PEOPLE COULD GET YOUR BOOK & READ IT. I WILL MAKE SURE I ALLOW PEOPLE TO READ THE ONE I HAVE ALSO

THANK YOU

COULD YOU PLEASE SEND ME ANY OTHER READING MATERIAL THAT WOULD BENIFIT MY WALK WITH JESUS.

Prison Evangelism, Inc. 510 Bering Dr. Suite 300 Houston Texas 77057

5/30/20

Thanks alot, form Eric ▨,

I'll be getting out soon, and I've got your Book and it just seem like it was for me, thanks for all the good things your doing.

its my first time in prison and last time, with Jesus Christ living in me I'll do good and out of trible thank you!!!

Hope you like it →

What Chaplains Say About the Books

TO: Prison Evangelism

FROM: Wayne Jefferson, Chaplain

DATE: June 25, 2018

RE: Labor of Love Book Donations

Marshall County Correctional Facility

833 West Street
Holly Springs, MS 38635

Thank you for the labor of love that you have displayed towards us by sending the books.

Many offenders and staff have benefited from this. Together, we have reached many hearts with the glorious gospel of Christ.

Our prayer is that you may continue to grow in the grace and knowledge of Him. May the Lord continue to bless you and make you a blessing.

In Christ,

Wayne L. Jefferson

Wayne Jefferson, Chaplain

72019

Seeking God — THROUGH PRAYER AND MEDITATION

I want to dig a little deeper. Please sender a free copy of "SEEKING GOD THROUGH PRAYER AND MEDITATION".

Commission Ministries Library
Chaplain D. Kelly
PO Box 180191
Fort Smith, AR 72908
Phone (479) 883-4872

Please tell us what you think of "How To Be A Child Of God". _____

Hi, Chaplain Kelly here. I would be interested in receiving Bulk Price on your Book "How to be a Child of God." Our ministry is presently sending Christian Books into about every Prison, jail & Juvenile in all 50 States. We're going back now for the 2nd time. Send list & Price of your Books. Thanks

Prison Evangelism, Inc. PO Box 571977 Houston Texas 77257

72019

Seeking God — THROUGH PRAYER AND MEDITATION

I want to dig a little deeper. Please sender a free copy of "SEEKING GOD THROUGH PRAYER AND MEDITATION".

Name Chaplain Susan Stout
Address PO Box 2000
City, State, Zip Wartburg, TN 37887
MCCX
(Morgan County Correctional Complex)

Please tell us what you think of "How To Be A Child Of God". _____

Many inmates have given very positive feedback about this book. Would love to see the next one so I can encourage them to order it for themselves. Thanks for all you do to build the Kingdom of God.

Prison Evangelism, Inc. PO Box 571977 Houston Texas 77257

What Chaplains Say About the Books

MILWAUKEE COUNTY SHERIFF'S OFFICE
949 N. 9TH STREET
MILWAUKEE, WI 53233

August 12th, 2020

Dear Mr. Howell,

Thank you so much for generously donating the new Spanish versions of the How to be a child of God book, to the Milwaukee County Jail. Now more than ever, our inmates need these resources in an environment of extended isolation during the COVID-19 crisis. The material you sent will go to very good use and is much needed. Our programming could not survive without help from people like you.

Thank you,

Officer Matthew Johnston
Program Coordinator
Milwaukee County Sheriff's Office
Milwaukee County Jail
949 N 9th Street
Milwaukee, WI   53233
(414) 226-7020
matthew.johnston@milwaukeecountywi.gov

David Howell
510 Bering Suite 300
Houston, Texas 77057

To whom it may concern,

I am writing on behalf of the Mt. Pleasant Correctional Facility. We really do appreciate How to be a child of God books that you have sent us. The inmates are doing great with the information in the book. We can't seem to keep them on our shelves. We would like to thank you for the books you have previously sent at no cost.

In the past we have received the following studies listed below and would greatly appreciate if your services could help us restock these.

May the Lord bless you for your service to him

Thank you in advance for any material that you can provide

We have received the following items In the past from you.

    A. **How to be a child of God**

    B. **Any other Christian books**

Respectfully,

Cory Holloway
MPCF Chaplain
(319) 385-9511 ext.2220
Cory.Holloway@iowa.gov

What Chaplains Say About the Books

STATE OF OKLAHOMA

OKLAHOMA DEPARTMENT OF CORRECTIONS
UNIT NAME

September 17, 2019

Dear Prison Evangelism:

Thanks for the 300 books you just donated. We love the books.

Would it be possible to send 700 more so we could put one for each inmate in their Christmas gift bags? That way, these books could get to inmates who would not normally come to the Chapel, but they will all get a gift bag.

Our female inmate population here at Eddie Warrior is at 952.

If you can't I fully understand. Thanks for your consideration.

Sincerely,

Kathryn McCollum
Chaplain/Volunteer Coordinator

MAILING ADDRESS
CITY, STATE ZIP
TELEPHONE NUMBER
FAX NUMBER
http://doc.ok.gov

What Chaplains Say About the Books

From: **Jewel Sensenig** sfpmjds@gmail.com
Subject: Re: Spanish version
Date: July 20, 2020 at 1:09 PM
To: David Howell davidhowell@prisonevangelism.com

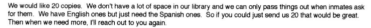

Lancaster County Prison
Attn: Chaplain's Office
625 E King St
Lancaster, PA 17602

We would like 20 copies. We don't have a lot of space in our library and we can only pass things out when inmates ask for them. We have English ones but just need the Spanish ones. So if you could just send us 20 that would be great. Then when we need more, I'll reach out to you again.

Thanks so much!!

On Mon, Jul 20, 2020 at 1:59 PM David Howell <davidhowell@prisonevangelism.com> wrote:
Please send your physical address. How many beds do you have?
David Howell
Prison Evangelism, Inc.
PO Box 571977
Houston, Texas 77257
713-623-0690
www.prisonevangelism.com

On Jul 20, 2020, at 12:25 PM, Jewel Sensenig <sfpmjds@gmail.com> wrote:

Hi David,

I'm writing from Lancaster County Prison. I had emailed you in March and you were out of Spanish versions of "How to be a child of God" but said to check in with you after June. Have the spanish ones been printed yet?

We would love to have 20 of them if they are available. Let me know.

Thanks!

--
Jewel Sensenig
Chaplain's Office Administrative Assistant
Lancaster County Prison/Support for Prison Ministries
sfpmjds@gmail.com

--
Jewel Sensenig
Chaplain's Office Administrative Assistant
Lancaster County Prison/Support for Prison Ministries
sfpmjds@gmail.com

What Chaplains Say About the Books

From: **Jeff Ruge** jaruge52@msn.com
Subject: How To Be A Child of God books
Date: October 5, 2019 at 4:29 PM
To: davidhowell@prisonevangelism.com

David, I'm sorry for the delay with this e-mail, You and I spoke on Wednesday afternoon around 3 p.m. about your publication "How To Be a Child of God".
I serve with four other Chaplains at Stateville NRC prison in Crest Hill, Illinois. NRC is the Northern Reception Center for the norther 1/2 of Illinois. The materials dispensed here travel throughout Illinois to the other facilities.

We are blessed to be accepted into this institution twice a week, able to speak into the lives to as many as 100 men per day. We are blessed to have other materials in our possession
that may very well trigger the heart to the change.

But, your book/booklet (when available) speaks to these men at a very emotion and heartfelt ways.

You mentioned that my request would yield a response. I mentioned in our phone conversation that we would be appreciative to obtain 200 or more, copies of your publications.

If you are still willing to share, you can send them to the following:
Chaplain Jeff Ruge
1184 Kingsley Lane
Aurora, IL. 60505

Thank you in advance for your response.

I shared the personal video from the CBN with my co-Chaplains. Your witness demonstrates that our Lord can use anyone of us in magnificent ways. All we have to be is open to the movement of the Spirit. You sir, have been moved by the Spirit to compose such an useful publication to provoke the heart to change.

I also asked if you had personal testimonies/letters of men that have been effected by your publication. You said you had many letters of personal affirmations. Those letters could serve as a   powerful affirmation for others. What we all have to understand is that our Lord does not discriminate, what He has done for one, He will do for another.
We are that other.

Thank you in advance for your response.

Blessings to you and your ministry.

Jeff Ruge

What Chaplains Say About the Books

Brother David Howell:

Hello! My name is Ray Lucero and I am the Senior Pastor of the newly formed <u>Central Fellowship</u> church at the correctional facility in Los Lunas, New Mexico. Myself and 6 other men volunteered to be transferred to this facility after graduating from the seminary program in Hobbs New Mexico and our mission to is evangelize and fulfill the Secretary of Corrections' vision of changing the prison culture from within. We are inmate chaplains here and because this facility is the **Reception and Diagnostic Center** for the *entire* Department of Corrections, every man must come through this facility. The average length of stay is only 6 weeks, with the exception of the Mental Health Unit, the Long-term Health unit, and the Segregation units. Needless to say, our facility is one always in transition. The need for Bibles, Bible studies and other ministry materials constant and when we received your book **"How to be a child of God,"** we were exceptionally blessed to have this book to give to the men passing through these doors that would help guide them through the process of becoming and being a man of God. We are already in need of more these books. We'd like to request at least 600-1000 copies of your book so that we have enough fill the need at this facility. If you have knowledge of ministries who can perhaps donate Bibles for our church we'd appreciate your assistance.

Thank you again. I hope that we can correspond and you can get to know our heart for the men in the New Mexico prison system. God changed our lives and has given us a heart to do the same for others. But without brothers like yourself, we'd sure have a hard time keeping these me occupied with Biblical reading. I look forward to hearing from you and future fellowship and praise reports. May God bless you abundantly above and beyond your biggest thoughts...

Sincerely,

Ray Lucero

Ray Lucero, Senior Pastor, Central Fellowship Church, CNMCF

Central Fellowship Church
Central New Mexico Correctional Facility
Jake Silva, Group Liaison
1525 Morris Rd.
Los Lunas, NM   87031

What Chaplains Say About the Books

**Kyle Correctional
Center**

23001 IH-35
Kyle, Texas 78640
Phone: 512-268-0079
Fax: 512-268-0366

David Howell Ministries
1535 West Loop South Suite 200
Houston, TX 77027

Dear David Howell Ministries Staff,

Greetings in the wonderful name of Jesus! I trust this letter finds you blessed and enjoying all the goodness of our Lord! Thank you for the generous donation of 100 copies of your evangelism book. I have received them in perfect condition and all will be used for the evangelism and discipleship of the men here. Thank you for your generosity and concern for the incarcerated. May God bless you richly!

Born Again To Win,

Michael R. McComb
Michael R. McComb, Chaplain

What Chaplains Say About the Books

Texas Department of Criminal Justice
Institutional Division

Price Daniel Unit

July 6, 2012

David Howell
How to be a Child of God
1535 West Loop South, Suite 200
Houston, Texas
77027

Dear Brother David,

I want to thank you for your recent phone call and for all of the 125 copies
of *How to be a Child of God* that arrived yesterday. I will put them out
this weekend for Chapel services and they will be snatched up for sure!

Please keep up the good work and thank you for caring for the men here at
the Price Daniel Unit.

Chaplain George Hanson
Price Daniel Unit
938 South FM 1673
Snyder, TX 79549

325-573-1114

What Chaplains Say About the Books

Halawa Correctional Facility
Chapel
99-902 Moanalua Road, Aiea Hawaii 96701
Ph: (808) 485-1884; email:gentledoveministries@ymail.com

April 21, 2016

Chaplain Charles Noland Jr.
Halawa Correctional Facility
99-902 Moanalua Rd.
Aiea, Hawaii 96701

Prison Evangelist Inc.
510 Bering, Suite 300
Houston, Texas 77057

Aloha Prison Evangelist Inc.:

We just received your generous donation of "How to be a Child of God" Books. I cannot begin to express my heartfelt gratitude to your organization for this abundant blessing. We were in need of these Books. This is truly an answer to our prayers for materials that we could use to build Starter Kits/Packet as a follow-up for prisoners who have just received Christ Jesus as their Lord and Savior and also for those who require guidance in their walk with Christ. Jesus is mighty indeed.

Thank you, for all your support, we are truly blessed by your generous giving and pray that the Lord multiply your giving a hundred fold. The prison community here at Halawa Correctional Facility lives only on the donations we receive. Your giving of these valuable resources helps us to keep our men walking upright and growing in our Lord and Savior, Christ Jesus daily with your donations.

I pray the Lord continues to pour out His blessings upon your organization and all its staff, volunteers, and contributors in such a way that you will not be able to contain them. The Lord's Blessing, Peace and Mercy be with you always.

With Warmest Aloha,

Charles Noland Jr.

Chaplain Charles Noland Jr.

YHWH bless you, and keep you:
YHWH make His face shine upon you, and be gracious unto you:
YHWH lift up His countenance upon you, and give you peace. (Num. 6:24-26)

What Chaplains Say About the Books

"HOPE" Prison Ministry, Inc.

Remember those in prison as if you were their fellow prisoners,
and those who are mistreated as if you yourselves were suffering.

Hebrews 13:3

August 2, 2018

Prison Evangelism
P.O. Box 571977
Houston, Texas 77257

Dear brother in Christ:

The booklets we ordered from you, "How to be a child of God," have really proven to be of great value to us.

The inmates are used to our handing out printed lessons that contain all of the verses we will be covering that day. This gets them used to not bringing their Bibles to the study.

But since we started using your booklet, 18 out of the 20 who normally attend brought their Bibles. NY only allows 20 individuals to go to a meeting at one time.

We have enclosed $200 to cover the cost of 100 booklets. It is my prayer that the booklets arrive quickly as we seem to be going through them quickly.

Keep up the good work.

Serving Him,

Chaplain Donald C. Watts
Founder, Director

P.O. Box 2611, Glenville, NY 12325
Telephone & Fax - (518) 384-1726 • Email: hopepm@nycap.rr.com • www.hopepm.com

What Chaplains Say About the Books

Arkansas Department of Correction

honor and integrity in public service

Varner Chapel
P.O. Box 600
Grady, AR 71644-0600
Phone: (870) 575-1800
Fax: (870) 479-3803
www.state.ar.us/doc

To David Howell

We have on average 1700 men at our unit. We are constantly having new men come in. We have used up the supply of illustrated books you sent us, "How to be a Child of God". Will you Please send us another 150 copies in English and 25 in Spanish. Thank you for working with us in spreading God's word and teaching men how to be men of God.

Sincerely In Christ

Sean Treas

An Equal Opportunity Employer

115

Bible Verses Used in The Book

The following verses have been referenced in this book. They are quoted here from the *New Living Translation*, which is the version I use in the booklets.

Acts 8:3 *But Saul was going everywhere to destroy the church. He went from house to house, dragging out both men and women to throw them into prison.*

Acts 9:1-2 *Meanwhile, Saul was uttering threats with every breath and was eager to kill the Lord's followers. So he went to the high priest. He requested letters addressed to the synagogues in Damascus, asking for their cooperation in the arrest of any followers of the Way he found there. He wanted to bring them—both men and women—back to Jerusalem in chains.*

Acts 11:7-9, 15-17 *And I heard a voice say, "Get up, Peter; kill and eat them." "No, Lord," I replied. "I have never eaten anything that our Jewish laws have declared impure or unclean." But the voice from heaven spoke again: "Do not call something unclean if God has made it clean." … "As I began to speak," Peter continued, "the Holy Spirit fell on [the Gentiles], just as he fell on us at the beginning. Then I thought of the Lord's words when he said, 'John baptized with water, but you will be baptized with the Holy Spirit.' And since God gave these Gentiles the same gift he gave us when we believed in the Lord Jesus Christ, who was I to stand in God's way?"*

Acts 22:3 *Then Paul said, "I am a Jew, born in Tarsus, a city in Cilicia, and I was brought up and educated here in Jerusalem under Gamaliel. As his student, I was carefully trained in our Jewish laws and customs. I became very zealous to honor God in everything I did, just like all of you today."*

Colossians 1:13 *For he has rescued us from the kingdom of darkness and transferred us into the Kingdom of his dear Son,*

Colossians 1:24-27 *I am glad when I suffer for you in my body, for I am participating in the sufferings of Christ that continue for his body, the church. God has given me the responsibility of serving his church by proclaiming his entire message to you. This message was kept secret for centuries and generations past, but now it has been revealed to God's people. For God wanted them to know that the riches and glory of Christ are for you Gentiles, too. And this is the secret: Christ lives in you. This gives you assurance of sharing his glory.*

Colossians 2:6 *And now, just as you accepted Christ Jesus as your Lord, you must continue to follow him.*

Colossians 2:12-13 *For you were buried with Christ when you were baptized. And with him you were raised to new life because you trusted the mighty power of God, who raised Christ from the dead. You were dead because of your sins and because your sinful nature was not yet cut away. Then God made you alive with Christ, for he forgave all our sins.*

Bible Verses Used in The Book

Colossians 3:1 *Since you have been raised to new life with Christ, set your sights on the realities of heaven, where Christ sits in the place of honor at God's right hand.*

Colossians 3:3-4 *For you died to this life, and your real life is hidden with Christ in God. And when Christ, who is your life, is revealed to the whole world, you will share in all his glory.*

1 Corinthians 2:2 *For I decided that while I was with you I would forget everything except Jesus Christ, the one who was crucified.*

1 Corinthians 6:15 *Don't you realize that your bodies are actually parts of Christ? Should a man take his body, which is part of Christ, and join it to a prostitute? Never!*

1 Corinthians 6:17 *But the person who is joined to the Lord is one spirit with him.*

1 Corinthians 12:12 *The human body has many parts, but the many parts make up one whole body. So it is with the body of Christ.*

1 Corinthians 12:18-23 *But our bodies have many parts, and God has put each part just where he wants it. How strange a body would be if it had only one part! Yes, there are many parts, but only one body. The eye can never say to the hand, "I don't need you." The head can't say to the feet, "I don't need you." In fact, some parts of the body that seem weakest and least important are actually the most necessary. And the parts we regard as less honorable are those we clothe with the greatest care. So we carefully protect those parts that should not be seen,*

1 Corinthians 15:3-4 *I passed on to you what was most important and what had also been passed on to me. Christ died for our sins, just as the Scriptures said. He was buried, and he was raised from the dead on the third day, just as the Scriptures said.*

2 Corinthians 5:7 *For we live by believing and not by seeing.*

2 Corinthians 5:14 *Either way, Christ's love controls us. Since we believe that Christ died for all, we also believe that we have all died to our old life.*

2 Corinthians 5:17-18 *This means that anyone who belongs to Christ has become a new person. The old life is gone; a new life has begun! And all of this is a gift from God, who brought us back to himself through Christ. And God has given us this task of reconciling people to him.*

2 Corinthians 5:21 *For God made Christ, who never sinned, to be the offering for our sin, so that we could be made right with God through Christ.*

Ephesians 1:7 *He is so rich in kindness and grace that he purchased our freedom with the blood of his Son and forgave our sins.*

Bible Verses Used in The Book

Ephesians 2:1 *Once you were dead because of your disobedience and your many sins.*

Ephesians 2:6 *For he raised us from the dead along with Christ and seated us with him in the heavenly realms because we are united with Christ Jesus.*

Ephesians 2:8-9 *God saved you by his grace when you believed. And you can't take credit for this; it is a gift from God. Salvation is not a reward for the good things we have done, so none of us can boast about it.*

Ephesians 2:10 *For we are God's masterpiece. He has created us anew in Christ Jesus, so we can do the good things he planned for us long ago.*

Ephesians 4:24 *Put on your new nature, created to be like God—truly righteous and holy.*

Ezekiel 36:26-27 *And I will give you a new heart, and I will put a new spirit in you. I will take out your stony, stubborn heart and give you a tender, responsive heart. And I will put my Spirit in you so that you will follow my decrees and be careful to obey my regulations.*

Galatians 1:15-16 *But even before I was born, God chose me and called me by his marvelous grace. Then it pleased him to reveal his Son to me so that I would proclaim the Good News about Jesus to the Gentiles.*

Galatians 1:17 *Nor did I go up to Jerusalem to consult with those who were apostles before I was. Instead, I went away into Arabia, and later I returned to the city of Damascus.*

Galatians 2:16-21 *Yet we know that a person is made right with God by faith in Jesus Christ, not by obeying the law. And we have believed in Christ Jesus, so that we might be made right with God because of our faith in Christ, not because we have obeyed the law. For no one will ever be made right with God by obeying the law." But suppose we seek to be made right with God through faith in Christ and then we are found guilty because we have abandoned the law. Would that mean Christ has led us into sin? Absolutely not! Rather, I am a sinner if I rebuild the old system of law I already tore down. For when I tried to keep the law, it condemned me. So I died to the law—I stopped trying to meet all its requirements—so that I might live for God. My old self has been crucified with Christ. It is no longer I who live, but Christ lives in me. So I live in this earthly body by trusting in the Son of God, who loved me and gave himself for me. I do not treat the grace of God as meaningless. For if keeping the law could make us right with God, then there was no need for Christ to die.*

Galatians 2:20 *My old self has been crucified with Christ. It is no longer I who live, but Christ lives in me. So I live in this earthly body by trusting in the Son of God, who loved me and gave himself for me.*

Bible Verses Used in The Book

Galatians 3:1-5 *Oh, foolish Galatians! Who has cast an evil spell on you? For the meaning of Jesus Christ's death was made as clear to you as if you had seen a picture of his death on the cross. Let me ask you this one question: Did you receive the Holy Spirit by obeying the law of Moses? Of course not! You received the Spirit because you believed the message you heard about Christ. How foolish can you be? After starting your new lives in the Spirit, why are you now trying to become perfect by your own human effort? Have you experienced so much for nothing? Surely it was not in vain, was it? I ask you again, does God give you the Holy Spirit and work miracles among you because you obey the law? Of course not! It is because you believe the message you heard about Christ.*

Galatians 3:11 *So it is clear that no one can be made right with God by trying to keep the law. For the Scriptures say, "It is through faith that a righteous person has life."*

Galatians 3:21 *Is there a conflict, then, between God's law and God's promises? Absolutely not! If the law could give us new life, we could be made right with God by obeying it.*

Hebrews 1:3 *The Son radiates God's own glory and expresses the very character of God, and he sustains everything by the mighty power of his command. When he had cleansed us from our sins, he sat down in the place of honor at the right hand of the majestic God in heaven.*

Hebrews 9:26 *If that had been necessary, Christ would have had to die again and again, ever since the world began. But now, once for all time, he has appeared at the end of the age to remove sin by his own death as a sacrifice.*

Hebrews 10:38 *"And my righteous ones will live by faith."*

Hebrews 13:3 *Remember those in prison, as if you were there yourself. Remember also those being mistreated, as if you felt their pain in your own bodies.*

James 1:18 *He chose to give birth to us by giving us his true word. And we, out of all creation, became his prized possession.*

John 1:1-2 *In the beginning the Word already existed. The Word was with God, and the Word was God. He existed in the beginning with God.*

John 1:12-13 *But to all who believed him and accepted him, he gave the right to become children of God. They are reborn—not with a physical birth resulting from human passion or plan, but a birth that comes from God.*

John 1:14 *So the Word became human and made his home among us. He was full of unfailing love and faithfulness. And we have seen his glory, the glory of the Father's one and only Son.*

Bible Verses Used in The Book

John 3:3-5 *Jesus replied, "I tell you the truth, unless you are born again, you cannot see the Kingdom of God." "What do you mean?" exclaimed Nicodemus. "How can an old man go back into his mother's womb and be born again?" Jesus replied, "I assure you, no one can enter the Kingdom of God without being born of water and the Spirit."*

John 5:18 *So the Jewish leaders tried all the harder to find a way to kill him. For he not only broke the Sabbath, he called God his Father, thereby making himself equal with God.*

John 10:10 *"The thief's purpose is to steal and kill and destroy. My purpose is to give them a rich and satisfying life."*

John 10:30-33 *"The Father and I are one." Once again the people picked up stones to kill him. Jesus said, "At my Father's direction I have done many good works. For which one are you going to stone me?" They replied, "We're stoning you not for any good work, but for blasphemy! You, a mere man, claim to be God."*

John 14:20 *"When I am raised to life again, you will know that I am in my Father, and you are in me, and I am in you."*

John 17:21 *I pray that they will all be one, just as you and I are one—as you are in me, Father, and I am in you. And may they be in us so that the world will believe you sent me.*

1 John 3:7 *Dear children, don't let anyone deceive you about this: When people do what is right, it shows that they are righteous, even as Christ is righteous.*

Luke 4:18 *"The Spirit of the LORD is upon me, for he has anointed me to bring Good News to the poor. He has sent me to proclaim that captives will be released, that the blind will see, that the oppressed will be set free . . ."*

Mark 5:18-20 *As Jesus was getting into the boat, the man who had been demon possessed begged to go with him. But Jesus said, "No, go home to your family, and tell them everything the Lord has done for you and how merciful he has been." So the man started off to visit the Ten Towns of that region and began to proclaim the great things Jesus had done for him; and everyone was amazed at what he told them.*

Matthew 11:28-30 *Then Jesus said, "Come to me, all of you who are weary and carry heavy burdens, and I will give you rest. Take my yoke upon you. Let me teach you, because I am humble and gentle at heart, and you will find rest for your souls. For my yoke is easy to bear, and the burden I give you is light."*

2 Peter 1:3 *By his divine power, God has given us everything we need for living a godly life. We have received all of this by coming to know him, the one who called us to himself by means of his marvelous glory and excellence.*

Bible Verses Used in The Book

Philippians 2:13 *For God is working in you, giving you the desire and the power to do what pleases him.*

Philippians 3:6 *I was so zealous that I harshly persecuted the church. And as for righteousness, I obeyed the law without fault.*

Romans 1:17 *This Good News tells us how God makes us right in his sight. This is accomplished from start to finish by faith. As the Scriptures say, "It is through faith that a righteous person has life."*

Romans 4:7-8 *"Oh, what joy for those whose disobedience is forgiven, whose sins are put out of sight. Yes, what joy for those whose record the LORD has cleared of sin."*

Romans 6:4 *For we died and were buried with Christ by baptism. And just as Christ was raised from the dead by the glorious power of the Father, now we also may live new lives.*

Romans 6:6-7 *We know that our old sinful selves were crucified with Christ so that sin might lose its power in our lives. We are no longer slaves to sin. For when we died with Christ we were set free from the power of sin.*

Romans 6:11-13 *So you also should consider yourselves to be dead to the power of sin and alive to God through Christ Jesus. Do not let sin control the way you live; do not give in to sinful desires. Do not let any part of your body become an instrument of evil to serve sin. Instead, give yourselves completely to God, for you were dead, but now you have new life. So use your whole body as an instrument to do what is right for the glory of God.*

Romans 7:4 *So, my dear brothers and sisters, this is the point: You died to the power of the law when you died with Christ. And now you are united with the one who was raised from the dead. As a result, we can produce a harvest of good deeds for God.*

Romans 7:22-23 *I love God's law with all my heart. But there is another power within me that is at war with my mind. This power makes me a slave to the sin that is still within me.*

Romans 8:1 *So now there is no condemnation for those who belong to Christ Jesus.*

Romans 10:9 *If you openly declare that Jesus is Lord and believe in your heart that God raised him from the dead, you will be saved.*

Romans 10:17 *So faith comes from hearing, that is, hearing the Good News about Christ.*

Romans 15:3 *For even Christ didn't live to please himself. As the Scriptures say, "The insults of those who insult you, O God, have fallen on me."*

HOW TO BE

...A Child Of
God

Witness Edition
Includes: *How to Tell Your Story* and *How to Witness*

How to Be a Child of God

David Howell

Support this Ministry

Prison Evangelism prints and distributes How to be a child of God free to 2100 prisons in the US representing 2,000,000 captives. Our purpose is to change hearts and close prisons. This is accomplished by trusting and love in Jesus Christ. Without a change of heart seventy percent will return to captivity within five years.

Help us set the captives free permanently by giving your financial support.

You can buy books for your own ministry by purchasing at:
howtobeachildofgod.com
All profits buy more books for prisons.

You can donate directly to this ministry at: **prisonevangelism.com**

Facebook: @ Prison Evangelism, Inc. and @How to be a child of God

You can also mail a check to: Prison Evangelism
                                 PO Box 571977
                                 Houston, Texas 77257

Copyright © 2019 by David Howell
All rights reserved. No part of this publication may be reproduced in any form without written permission from David Howell

This title may be purchased in bulk for educational and evangelical purposes. Please contact the publisher for more information.

David Howell
PO Box 571977
Houston, Texas 77257
davidhowell@aol.com
info@HowtobeaChildofGod.com
www.HowtobeaChildofGod.com

SEE THIS EBOOK AND WATCH THIS VIDEO
@ WWW.PRISONEVANGELISM.COM

Unless otherwise indicated, all Scripture quotations are taken from the Holy Bible, New Living Translation, copyright © 1996, 2004, 2007 by Tyndale House Foundation. Used by permission of Tyndale House Publishers, Inc., Carol Stream, Illinois 60188. All rights reserved.

ISBN: 978-0-578-14157-2

Art direction by John Magee, Houston, Texas
JohnMageeDesign.com

All illustrations by Randy Rogers, The Woodlands, Texas
artistguy@att.net

INTRODUCTION

"In fact, if a full presentation of Christ and His Cross is made to us at the very outset, we may well step into a great deal of experience from the first day of our Christian life, even though the full explanation of much of it may only follow later."

Watchman Nee, The Normal Christian Life

When we trust Jesus Christ as Lord, God, Savior and Life, we are also asking Him to take over our will and our lives. In fact He becomes our life. We are transformed; sometimes quickly, sometimes slowly, but change always comes. The very Spirit of God comes to live in us and makes us whole, alive and complete. Life will never be the same when we believe and give our hearts to God.

David Howell

God was in the Heavens and came to earth as a man

Philippians 2:6-8, John 1:14, Hebrews 1:3, Romans 8:3b, John 10:30, Colossians 1:15, Colossians 2:9, Hebrews 2:11-17, Matthew 1:20-23

He was conceived in a miraculous way, but He was born of a woman in the same way we were.

He did this so that we could form a personal relationship with Him and know Him as both God and man and better understand Him as Father.

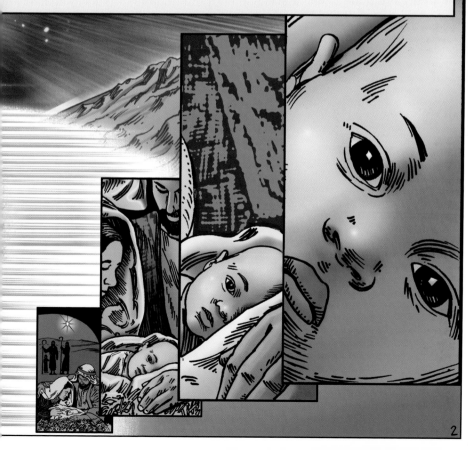

2

Jesus went through childhood and adolescence, learned a trade; and when His time came, He began the ministry that He had come to do, revealing Himself to all of us as God and Savior.

Matthew 3:13-17, Matthew 7:28-29, Mark 6:2-3, Luke 2:40, Luke 2:41-47, Luke 2:52

When His purpose on earth was complete, He allowed Himself to be crucified. He was humiliated and tortured and then nailed to a cross. Jesus chose to die this most brutal of deaths so you and I wouldn't have to pay the penalty for our wrongdoing. He wanted us to identify with Him and what He went through.

In ways known only to God, the sacrifice and the blood of Jesus Christ is able to wash away our sins and cleanse us forever. This total act of love gave us purity so God could see us as one of His children, just as He sees Jesus.

Matthew 26:28-29, Matthew 27:57- 61, Romans 5: 6, Romans 8:3, Ephesians 1:7, Hebrews 2:14 -15, Hebrews 9:22, 1 Peter 2:24, 1 John 1:7

After His death, Jesus was buried, and then God brought Him back to life. Many saw Him alive in the days following and then He returned to the Heavenly places.

Jesus came so that we could establish a personal relationship with Him and to give us His gift of eternal life. Eternal life is Christ's life. **It has no beginning, and it has no end.**

Luke 24:1-7, Luke 24:50-51, John 16:28, Hebrews 1:3

Why was all this necessary? Because when God created the first man, Adam, He gave him a wonderful life in Paradise, but Adam disobeyed his Heavenly Father.

Because of Adam's selfish act of disobedience, he was separated from God and died spiritually.

From that point, man had a body and soul (personality), but spiritually he was dead to God. He was not whole and could no longer experience the blessings God had in store.

Genesis 2:8-9, Genesis 3:2-6, Genesis 2:16-17, Genesis 3:23, I Corinthians 15:45-46

As a child of our parents with a family lineage going back to Adam, we died spiritually with Adam in the Garden of Eden.

We carry the burdens of that lineage, plus the burdens of our own sins and the emotional baggage we pick up in our lifetime on earth. It is a real bag of junk with shame, guilt, past problems and hang-ups, and bad feelings about our sins and character defects. We are in need of a new lineage and a new family.

Romans 3:23, Romans 5:12, Romans 5:18a

One day, someone came along and explained the story of Jesus, how He came to save each of us from eternal death by dying for us and giving us His eternal life. Jesus died, giving us all a way out, a way to experience total forgiveness, unconditional love, and hope of eternal life through Him.

Ezekiel 36:26-27, Acts 4:12, Romans 5:9, 1 Corinthians 15:57, 2 Corinthians 5:18a, Galatians1:15-16, Ephesians 2:8-9, 1 Timothy 2:5-6

Jesus also came so that you and I could have peace and an abundant life on this earth now through a relationship with Him. He wants to show us how to cope with life's problems. Jesus offers hope and a new design for living. Our natural ways keep us self-absorbed and in turmoil. They have not worked.

John 10:10, Romans 6:16, Romans 6:21, Romans 8:37, Ephesians 2:14, Revelation 3:20

We cannot have peace when we are separated from God. The choices, the ones we make every day, are self-centered and keep us frustrated and separated from fellowship with God. We have a deep yearning for a peaceful union with our Heavenly Father, but we lack that spiritual connection. Our own best thinking and good intentions got us into this mess.

Ecclesiastes 3:11, Romans 6:16, Luke 1:78-79, John 16:33, Romans 5:1-2, Romans 8:6

10

We attempt to bridge the gap that separates us from God, and we seek ways to reestablish a relationship with Him. None work. Only through trust in Jesus Christ can we get in touch with God the Father.

Proverbs 14:12, Romans 6:23, Romans 3:23

This is the same Jesus who died for all of our sins, faults, and character defects; past, present and future. Through His blood, we can be cleansed and made right before God. We can receive total forgiveness and unconditional love from God the Father. With His death and return to life, Jesus bridged the gap between God and man. That is why He is the Savior of the World.

John 3:16, I Peter 3:18, I Timothy 2:5-6, Romans 5:1

We all have an opportunity to accept or reject this truth. If we accept these events as true and trust in Jesus as God, we become children of God, with all the rights and privileges Jesus has. We become a co-heir and a brother or sister of Jesus Christ. Turn your will and your lives over to His care with complete abandon. It is not complicated, but it may be one of the most difficult things you have ever done. If you truly want to experience the promises of God and the joy that comes from fellowship with Him, ask Him to take over your life. If you are sincere, the simplest of prayers is enough...because God sees your heart. Give yourself to Him with this simple prayer. THAT IS ALL THAT IS NEEDED WHEN YOU TRUST AND BELIEVE!

Ephesians 2:13, John 14:6, Hebrews 4:3, Hebrews 4:7

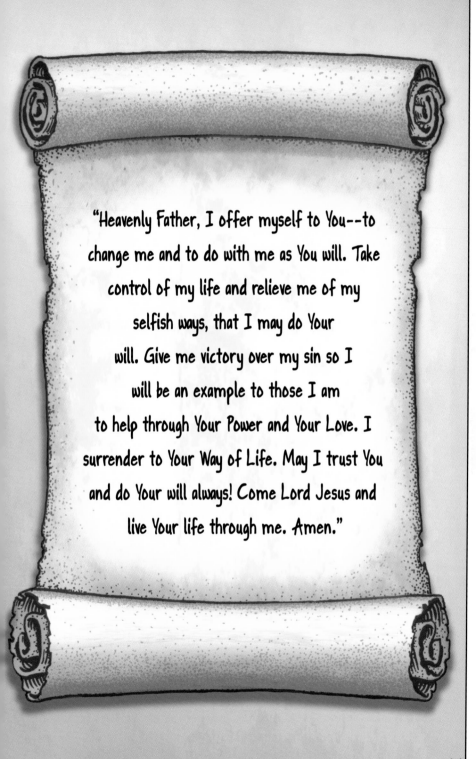

"Heavenly Father, I offer myself to You--to change me and to do with me as You will. Take control of my life and relieve me of my selfish ways, that I may do Your will. Give me victory over my sin so I will be an example to those I am to help through Your Power and Your Love. I surrender to Your Way of Life. May I trust You and do Your will always! Come Lord Jesus and live Your life through me. Amen."

Say with your mouth and believe in your heart that Jesus died, was buried, and came back to life. Trust in Him that He is Lord, Savior and God in the flesh and become a Child of God and co-heir with Christ.

John 11:25-26, John 14:6-7, Romans 10:9, Romans 10:13, 1 Corinthians 6:17, Ephesians 1:5-8, Ephesians 2:8-10, Colossians 2:6-7, 1 John 5:12-13

15

As you receive the Spirit of God, you become whole and alive to God.

16

When you ask Jesus Christ to come into your life, you ar
transferred out of the lineage of your earthly family
Adam and into the eternal life of Christ, **the life that**
forever in the past and forever in the future. You ar
transferred to the cross and the old self dies with Christ

Romans 5:18-19, Romans 8:1-2, 1 Corinthians 15:22, Galatians 5:24,
Ephesians 1:13-14, Ephesians 3:14-15, 1 Peter 1:18-19

u become one with Him. You are united with Christ, and
at will never change. Jesus now lives in you and you in
m. Wherever He goes, you go. Wherever you go, He goes.

John 14:20, Romans 6:6, Galatians 2:20, Galatians 4:4-7,
Galatians 5:24, Ephesians 1:11, Colossians 2:10

18

When your "old self" died with Jesus on the Cross, you also were buried with Him. Your new spiritual self comes to life with Christ and ascends into the Heavenly places with Him. You left behind the bag of shortcomings, guilt, sins and shame. You are in Christ, and He is in you. You exchange your old life for a new one. You now have the Spirit of God in you and your human spirit has been restored to life with God. You are in Christ and along for the great ride of your eternal life. YOU ARE REBORN!

John 3:6, John 11:25-26, Romans 5:5, Romans 6:4-6, Romans 8:10, Colossians 2:12-14, Colossians 3:1-3, Ephesians 1:13b, Ephesians 2:6

If you were sincere in your prayer, you are now a member of a new family -- the Family of God. God the Father adopts us all as His own children, and we become co-heirs with our older brother Jesus. He accepts you and loves you unconditionally as a part of His family, YOU ARE A CHILD OF GOD!

Psalm 16:11, Romans 5:11, Romans 8:15-17a, 2 Corinthians 5:17, Philippians 3:20a, Hebrews 2:11-12, Revelation 21:2

Your old self died on the cross along with the sin burdens Christ carried. You can be relieved that you no longer need be captive to the sins, addictions, and other selfish ways of man. You died with Christ and can no longer be threatened with death as Satan's weapon of fear is rendered ineffective.

A new courage and a new boldness come with this new eternal life. Death no longer has influence and mastery over you. Christ died for our sins of cheating, stealing, lying and a host of other things. We died with Him and we are released from the power sin held over us. We now have the freedom of choice to do things our way or God's way. We did not have this choice before we turned our will and our lives over to the care of God through Jesus Christ.

Romans 6:11-13, Romans 8:1-2, Romans 8:15-17a, Galatians 5:16, Colossians 2:6-7, 2 Timothy 1:7, Hebrews 2:14-15

It may be difficult for us to fully comprehend this truth since our bodies and souls---our personalities---are still living out this life on earth. But now the Spirit of God lives in us and we are spiritual beings. If we are to have the abundant life that God wants us to have, then we must accept these events by faith. Change your thinking and visualize who and where you are. Set your mind on Heavenly things with your Father and not on the garbage that exists in our daily lives on this earth. You will find pure gladness to be in the Family of God. Your old self died, and you have a new life in Jesus Christ. It is a whole new way of thinking. YOU ARE BEING TRANSFORMED!

Romans 8:5-6, Romans 12:2, 1 Corinthians 2:16, Ephesians 2:6, Philippians 2:5, Philippians 3:20a, Philippians 4:6-8, Colossians 3:1-3, 2 Timothy 1:7

Our heritage is either in the lineage of our biological parents and Adam, or it is in the Family of God. There are no other choices. Apart from faith in Jesus Christ, each of us remains in Adam.

Many believers think they can have one foot in the lineage of Adam (or the world of our earthly family) and the other foot in the Family of God. The result is inner conflict and spiritual turmoil. Failing to make a clear choice leaves us confused and short of the victory God has for us.

Matthew 7:13-14, Romans 6:16, Romans 7:14-25, Romans 8:1-2,
1 Corinthians 15:22, Galatians 5:16, Philippians 3:20

Just as God is in three persons, (Father, Son and Holy Spirit) we also are in three dimensions. We live in a body that relates to the environment through our senses. We have a soul that expresses our personality through our mind, will and emotions. And we are spirit, now awakened through our trust in Jesus and our union with His death on the cross, burial and resurrection. Our spiritual dimension is the part of us that relates to God.

Genesis 2:7, Matthew 3:13-17, John 3:6, Romans 8:10, 1 Corinthians 3:16 -18, 1 Thessalonians 5:23 -24, Hebrews 4:12

Our role is to be absolutely and totally surrendered to Jesus Christ. His desire is to live His life in us and through us in order to accomplish His purpose on this earth.

We literally are the Body of Christ, and He desires to use each of us to reach others and expand the Family. Welcome to the Family of God. You are a new creature! Say "good-bye" to the old self and "hello" to the new self, with Jesus Christ living in you.

Romans 6:11-13, Romans 8:10, Romans 12:1, Romans 12:4-5,
1 Corinthians 3:16, 1 Corinthians 6:19-20, 2 Corinthians 5:16-21,
Ephesians 4:21-24, Philippians 2:5-8, Colossians 1:27,
1 John 3:1-3, 1 John 3:9-10, 1 John 5:18-19

As a child of God and co-heir with Jesus, we begin to share an inheritance with Him and get a glimpse of abundant living. With His new spirit in you, you will want to learn more about God's ways so you can follow Him. God has revealed Himself most completely in His Son, Jesus. So learn all you can about Him. Get a Bible and read the New Testament about the life of Jesus. The Book of John is a good beginning. The first twelve chapters of Genesis in the Old Testament explains how it all began. Check the references at the bottom of the pages of this book with your own Bible or look up the Bible verses in the reference section of this book to better understand what is said on each page.

- Talk to your new Father every day in prayer. Thank Him for your new life and your new family. Talk to Him openly and intimately just like a friend, as if He were sitting beside you. Imagine Him in the form of Jesus, whom you can relate to as an older brother.
- Read the Bible. Now that you have a new spirit, with the Spirit of God in you, you will receive a new understanding of what the scripture means. Bible scripture is the Word of God and the way your new Father has of speaking to you. He loves you more than you can ever imagine.
- Find a church, congregation and/or a Bible study meeting where you can meet others and stay committed as you grow in your faith. Your Heavenly Father can also talk to you through other believers.
- Water Baptism should follow soon after your commitment to Jesus. It is an act of imitation, obedience, and identification with Him.
- Get a sponsor in the Christian faith, someone to disciple or mentor you whom you can learn from and be accountable to.
- Go tell others of your new faith and trust in Jesus.
- We recommend the purchase of a Bible. Such as, the Holy Bible, New Living Translation (NLT), Tyndale House Publishers, Inc.
God bless your spiritual journey!

Joshua 1:8, Matthew 3:13-17, Matthew 7:7-8, Matthew 10:32, John 14:13-14, John 15:7, Philippians 4:6-7, Hebrews 4:12, James 5:15-16, 1 John 1:9

Don't copy the behavior and customs of the world, but let God transform you into a new person by changing the way you think. Then you will learn to know God's will for you, which is good and pleasing and perfect.

Romans 12:2, NLT

Since I live, you also will live. When I am raised to life again, you will know that I am in My Father, and you are in Me, and I am in you.
John 14:19b-20, NLT

We were crucified with Him, buried with Him, raised with Him, and now we are seated with Him in the very presence of God.

For He raised us up from the dead along with Christ and seated us with Him in the Heavenly realms because we are united with Christ Jesus.

Ephesians 2:6, NLT

My old self has been crucified with Christ. It is no longer I who live, but Christ lives in me. So I live in this earthly body by trusting in the Son of God, who loved me and gave Himself for me.

Galatians 2:20, NLT

Now that you are a Child of God . . . .

As a new child of God, you have all the privileges of being His son or daughter. You get to fellowship with Him, call Him Father, sit in His lap, pour out your heart to Him and generally let Him be your ever-loving Dad, companion, friend, provider and confidante. Along with the privileges there are also responsibilities and some of these will be explained in the next few pages.

You are instructed to go and tell someone soon after you receive Christ.

Everyone who acknowledges me publicly here on earth, I will also acknowledge before my Father in heaven. Matthew 10:32

The problem is, we have not really been taught how to do that, but the process is simple and explained in the next few pages of **How to Tell Your Story.** The key is willingness and the concept is simple and easy if you were sincere when you prayed and asked Jesus to take over your will and your lives. He is in you at this moment making changes in the way you think, decide and feel. The concept is as plain as

I never cared about anything and now I do. I didn't know what love was and now I do...I'm changing.

I was blind and now I can see (John 9:25). When you tell your story, you are being obedient and doing what God wants you to do. You are embarking on your new life. Remember, it is not you, but Christ in you, so be willing and let Him speak.

. . . . Pass it on!

We are also charged to bring others to know Jesus Christ and expand the Kingdom of God. (**For the Son of Man came to seek and save those who are lost. Luke 19:10.**) You are the body of Christ and can carry this out with the instructions on the next few pages. The key is availability. You must make yourself available so that Jesus Christ can live His life through you to reach these others. He may not be asking you to go out and speak to strangers, but to reach out to people you already know, see and visit on a day-to-day basis. He already has them picked out and when you think of someone that you imagine may want to know Jesus, you are beginning to think with the mind of Christ. The section **How to Witness** teaches you how to lead someone to know Jesus Christ and have peace with God. The instructions are not difficult. All it requires is willingness on your part and the desire to allow Jesus Christ to live His life through you.

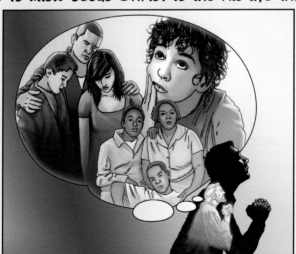

I urge you, first of all, to pray for all people. Ask God to help them: intercede on their behalf, and give thanks for them. 1 Timothy 2:1

I was blind, and now I can see! John 9:25

How to Tell Your Story
Christian Witness through Personal Testimony

Sharing your personal testimony of coming to know and trust Jesus Christ is the first step in practicing personal evangelism. There are two types of personal testimony. One is historical, which is telling about your life before, during and after the time you came to trust Jesus Christ as Lord and God, and Savior of your soul. The other is a theme type testimony and might simply be the event of your salvation and what life has been like since that time. This could be for someone who came to Christ as a child and might report of his life since conversion. Another example could be a person who had believed he was a Christian all his life but found he really didn't know God and then came to the point of surrender and repentance.

BEGIN THE TESTIMONY BY MENTIONING SOME COMMON GROUND YOU AND YOUR SUBJECT SHARE; SAME HOMETOWN, SAME JOB, SAME SCHOOL, ETC. FIND SOME MUTUAL INTERESTS.

How it Was

In telling your story, you recount and briefly tell of the road that led you to want to change the way you think and manage your life. All of us have made bad decisions and wrong choices in life that we wish we had not made and would like to do over again. If only we had the opportunity and the chance to live it again. Sometimes, it is a series of events that sets us back or it can be one major mistake or an unexpected event that can cause us to rethink our lives. Whatever the circumstance, the consequence of our actions or behavior can be the catalyst that brings us to the end of self. That is when you know that you can no longer operate in the same way and a change must take place or there will be a serious price to pay. You might have already reached the point where you are paying the consequences. Many of us get to a place in our life journey when we know we can no longer rely on self. Self is not getting the job done. We need to find out who is the real God and quit playing the role.

What Happened

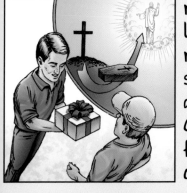

When we have humbled ourselves and find we are not masters of the universe, we begin to look at our options. In a strange and miraculous way, a proclaimer appears, someone who tells us about a better and everlasting life and peace with God. It might be in the form of a friend or a relative or a child, brother or sister or friend. He might ask you

34

to church or a Bible study. He might witness to you (through his own personal testimony) and suggest you try a more spiritual approach to your problems, like seeking Jesus first and admitting your lack of power to carry on as before. But something gets your attention as you seek God and you are ready at last to surrender and to accept

a new way of life. You want to become a child of God and in all of the forms that can be achieved. It happens to you. You have come to trust the Lord Jesus Christ and have asked Him to take over your will and your lives. The new life has begun.

How it is Now

You became a child of God, a born again believer. You have come to love and trust the Lord Jesus Christ as Lord, God, Savior and Life. Your life is changed and you are on track with a new attitude and a new set of values. You are now account-able to your heavenly Father. In this section you recount the ways your life has been altered and your thinking and even your personality have changed. Explain how God's grace is equipping you to deal with the difficulties of life and how the Spirit of God prompts you to do the right thing and corrects you when you are heading down the wrong path. You can explain the good and the bad in this section. We know it is not always good. The important thing is that the **Christ in you** is doing a work and you are the work in progress.

What Next

We grow in Christ from here on. Sometimes the road is bumpy and full of potholes, but we have new tools to cope with the obstacles and problems we encounter. We have the power of God through the Holy Spirit within us to show us the way and keep us from making the wrong choices of the old life. We study the Bible and learn to imitate Christ by learning His ways and manners. We come to realize and understand that when Christ died, our old self died with Him and we are now new creatures. We just need to know and understand that Jesus Christ lives in us and appropriate that basic truth as we are being saved and transformed into His likeness. You begin to emulate the risen Savior as you mature as a Christian.

For, "Who can know the Lord's thoughts? Who knows enough to teach him?" But we understand these things, for we have the mind of Christ.
1 Corinthians 2:16

You begin to realize that Jesus Christ, the Living God is seeking to live His life in you and through you to accomplish His desires with those who are His, the children of God. **You are becoming more like Christ, leaving the past behind and following Him.**

Psalm 40:3, John 9:25, John 12:17, Colossians 4:5-6, 1 Thessalonians 1:6-8, 1 Peter 3:15, Revelation 12:11, Revelation 19:10

How to Witness
Instructions for introducing an unbeliever to Jesus Christ.

The following ten suggestions are an effective means for delivering the message of the cross. Follow the directions carefully and you will succeed. You will become an effective seed planter and soul winner. In any case, you will be engaged in expanding the kingdom of God and that is the primary purpose for your existence.

• **Think of ten people.** These might be friends, relatives, loved ones or people you deal with in business or everyday life where you shop, play and work.

• **Write down their names.** When you finish writing the ten special names down, tape the piece of paper somewhere you will be reminded of them every day.

• **Begin to pray for the salvation of each person.** As you pray, ask God to open their minds and hearts to hearing about Jesus and eternal life. Remember we are not seeking to make bad people good, but spiritually dead people alive by offering them the gift of eternal life that you received.

• **Continue praying for each one for twenty-one days.** God doesn't care about the measure of time you spend praying for these special souls, but we know it takes twenty one days to establish a habit. So, make sure you have prayed for these over that period of time. Then you will have established a powerful habit of praying for the lost.

• **Begin contacting each one.** After the twenty-one days, you will have covered your subjects with prayer and now is the time for action. Call the first one and tell him you have something to show him and you want to see if it makes sense. Invite your friend for coffee or lunch. Continue the calls or contacts until you get a 'Yes'.

• **Show the book** *HOW TO BE A CHILD OF GOD.* Tell your friend you saw this little book and it made an impact on you and you would like to see if it might mean anything to him. If you have a computer or iPad or other mobile device, you can go to: www.howtobeachildofgod.com and read the ebook or watch the video presentation if you don't have a copy of the actual book.

• **Go through the entire book page by page.** Read the prayer on page 14, but move on through to completion of the book. Show your friend the scriptures in the back of the booklet, explaining they are there for easy reference in case a Bible isn't available. Demonstrate how the verses explain or prove the text or illustration.

• **Tell your story.** At that point, start telling your story or testimony of how you came to know Jesus Christ. A testimony explains: HOW IT WAS, WHAT HAPPENED, HOW IT IS NOW. If you don't have a testimony that you can relate to someone else, you should read through the book privately, pray the prayer on page 14 out loud

Christ in You
Colossians 1:27

and believe what you have said in your heart. Then you can go back and continue the conversation. Check the article HOW TO TELL YOUR STORY: CHRISTIAN WITNESS THROUGH PERSONAL TESTIMONY that precedes these pages.

• **Ask a leading question.** Ask your friend if what you have said means anything to him. Ask him if he thinks he will go to heaven when he dies. Ask him what he thinks is the meaning of eternal life. Get him into a spiritual and Christ centered conversation. God will give you the words to say, you just need to be willing and open.

• **Lead your friend to know Jesus Christ.** If the person responds in a positive way, ("I want what you have. How do you become a Christian? I want to know more.") lead him to Christ by going back to the prayer on page 14 in HOW TO BE A CHILD OF GOD and let your friend pray through it aloud either by himself or repeating after you. After praying with him, go back over the text and pictures on pages 15-20 to make sure all is understood regarding the message of the cross. If you have been thorough, there will be a new name written down in glory and your friend will be a child of God!

Reaping the Harvest

If you follow these simple instructions, you will become a soul winner. There is no question or condition. God created you with a very distinct personality and sphere of influence designed to appeal to certain people that you already know. All you have to do is be prayed up and approach them. **He will do the rest!** Chances are, the very people you put on your list are the ones He has chosen as well. They only need a proclaimer and that would be you! **God will speak through you as you talk to your friend. Just believe the entire exercise has been designed ahead of time and God has been waiting for you to arrive.** Avail yourself and that is all our Father wants. The only condition is that the time may not be exactly right for that person to come to Christ.

In that case, you will not be a soul winner that day, but you will be a seed planter. Either way, you will be obedient to your Heavenly Father, and that is really all He asks. If you are a child of God, it is never you, but Christ in you that is taking care of the task.

Matthew 4:19-20, Matthew 10:32, Luke 9:60, Luke 10:2, Luke 19:10, John 15:16, Acts 1:8, Acts 9:28, 1 Timothy 2:3-4

Acts 1:8 But you will receive power when the Holy Spirit comes upon you. And you will be my witnesses, telling people about me everywhere---in Jerusalem, throughout Judea, in Samaria, and to the ends of the earth. Page 40

Acts 4:12 There is salvation in no one else! God has given no other name under heaven by which we must be saved." Page 8

Acts 9:28 So Saul stayed with the apostles and went all around Jerusalem with them, preaching boldly in the name of the Lord. Page 40

Colossians 1:15 Christ is the visible image of the invisible God. He existed before anything was created and is supreme over all creation. Pages 1 & 2

Colossians 1:27b And this is the secret: Christ lives in you. This gives you assurance of sharing his glory. Page 25

Colossians 2:6-7 And now, just as you accepted Christ Jesus as your Lord, you must continue to follow him. Let your roots grow down into him, and let your lives be built on him, then your faith will grow strong in the truth you were taught, and you will overflow with thankfulness. Pages 15 & 16

Colossians 2:9 For in Christ lives all the fullness of God in a human body. Pages 1 & 2

Colossians 2:10 So you also are complete through your union with Christ, who is the head over every ruler and authority. Page 18

Colossians 2:12-14 For you were buried with Christ when you were baptized. And with him you were raised to new life because you trusted the mighty power of God, who raised Christ from the dead. You were dead because of your sins and because your sinful nature was not yet cut away. Then God made you alive with Christ, for he forgave all our sins. He canceled the record of the charges against us and took it away by nailing it to the cross. Page 19

Colossians 3:1-3 Since you have been raised to new life with Christ, set your sights on the realities of heaven, where Christ sits in the place of honor at God's right hand. Think about the things of heaven, not the things of earth. For you died to this life, and your real life is hidden with Christ in God. Page 19

Colossians 4:5-6 Live wisely among those who are not believers, and make the most of every opportunity. Let your conversation be gracious and attractive so that you will have the right response for everyone. Page 36

1 Corinthians 2:16 For, "Who can know the LORD's thoughts? Who knows enough to teach him?" But we understand these things, for we have the mind of Christ. Page 22

1 Corinthians 3:16-18 Don't you realize that all of you together are the temple of God and that the Spirit of God lives in you? God will destroy anyone who destroys this temple. For God's temple is holy and you are that temple. Stop deceiving yourselves. If you think you are wise by this world's standards, you need to become a fool to be truly wise. Pages 24 & 25

1 Corinthians 6:17 But the person who is joined to the Lord is one spirit with him. Pages 15 & 16 & 24

1 Corinthians 6:19-20 Don't you realize that your body is the temple of the Holy Spirit, who lives in you and was given to you by God? You do not belong to yourself, for God bought you with a high price. So you must honor God with your body. Page 25

1 Corinthians 15:22 Just as everyone dies because we all belong to Adam, everyone who belongs to Christ will be given new life. Pages 17 & 23

1 Corinthians 15:45-46 The Scriptures tell us, "The first man, Adam, became a living person." But, the last Adam — that is, Christ — is a life-giving Spirit. What comes first is the natural body then the spiritual body comes later. Page 6

1 Corinthians 15:57 But thank God! He gives us victory over sin and death through our Lord Jesus Christ. Page 8

2 Corinthians 5:16-21 So we have stopped evaluating others from a human point of view. At one time we thought of Christ merely from a human point of view. How differently we know him now! This means that anyone who belongs to Christ has become a new person. The old life is gone; a new life has begun! And all of this is a gift from God, who brought us back to himself through Christ. And God has given us this task of reconciling people to him. For God

was in Christ, reconciling the world to himself, no longer counting people's sins against them. And he gave us this wonderful message of reconciliation. So we are Christ's ambassadors; God is making his appeal through us. We speak for Christ when we plead, "Come back to God!" For God made Christ, who never sinned, to be the offering for our sin, so that we could be made right with God through Christ. Page 25

2 Corinthians 5:17 This means that anyone who belongs to Christ has become a new person. The old life is gone; a new life has begun! Page 20

2 Corinthians 5:18 And all of this is a gift from God, who brought us back to himself through Christ. Page 8

Ecclesiastes 3:11 Yet God has made everything beautiful for its own time. He has planted eternity in the human heart, but even so, people cannot see the whole scope of God's work from beginning to end. Page 10

Ephesians 1:5-8 God decided in advance to adopt us into his own family by bringing us to himself hrough Jesus Christ. This is what he wanted to do, and it gave him great pleasure. So we praise God for the glorious grace he has poured out on us who belong to his dear Son. He is so rich in kindness and grace that he purchased our freedom with the blood of his Son and forgave our sins. He has showered his kindness on us, along with all wisdom and understanding. Pages 15 & 16

Ephesians 1:7 He is so rich in kindness and grace that he purchased our freedom with the blood of his Son and forgave our sins. Page 4

Ephesians 1:11 Furthermore, because we are united with Christ, we have received an inheritance from God, for he chose us in advance, and he makes everything work out according to his plan. Page 18

Ephesians 1:13-14 And now you Gentiles have also heard the truth, the Good News that God saves you. And when you believed in Christ, he identified you as his own by giving you the Holy Spirit, whom he promised long ago. The Spirit is God's guarantee that he will give us the inheritance he promised and that he has purchased us to be his own people. He did this so we would praise and glorify him. Pages 17 & 19

Ephesians 2:6 For he raised us from the dead along with Christ and seated us with him in the heavenly realms because we are united with Christ Jesus. Page 19

Ephesians 2:8-10 God saved you by his grace when you believed. And you can't take credit for this; it is a gift from God. Salvation is not a reward for the good things we have done, so none of us can boast about it. For we are God's masterpiece. He has created us anew in Christ Jesus, so we can do the good things he planned for us long ago. Pages 8 & 15 & 16

Ephesians 2:13 But now you have been united with Christ Jesus. Once you were far away from God, but now you have been brought near to him through the blood of Christ. Page 13

Ephesians 2:14 For Christ himself has brought peace to us. He united Jews and Gentiles into one people when, in his own body on the cross, he broke down the wall of hostility that separated us. Page 9

Ephesians 3:14-15 When I think of all this, I fall to my knees and pray to the Father, the Creator of everything in heaven and on earth. Page 17

Ephesians 4:21-22 Since you have heard about Jesus and have learned the truth that comes from him, throw off your old sinful nature and your former way of life, which is corrupted by lust and deception. Page 25

Ezekiel 36:26-27 And I will give you a new heart, and I will put a new spirit in you. I will take out your stony, stubborn heart and give you a tender, responsive heart. And I will put my Spirit in you so that you will follow my decrees and be careful to obey my regulations. Page 8

Galatians 1:15-16 But even before I was born, God chose me and called me by his marvelous grace. Then it pleased him to reveal his Son to me so that I would proclaim the Good News about Jesus to the Gentiles. Page 8

Galatians 2:20 My old self has been crucified with Christ. It is no longer I who live, but Christ lives in me. So I live in this earthly body by trusting in the Son of God, who loved me and gave himself for me. Page 18

Galatians 4:4-7 But when the right time came, God sent his Son, born of a woman, subject to the law. God sent him to buy freedom for us who were slaves to the law, so that he could adopt us as his very own children. And because we are his children, God has sent the Spirit of his Son into our hearts, prompting us to call out, "Abba, Father." Now you are no longer a slave but God's own child. And since you are his child, God has made you his heir. Page 18

Galatians 5:16 So I say, let the Holy Spirit guide your lives. Then you won't be doing what your sinful nature craves. Page 23

Galatians 5:24 Those who belong to Christ Jesus have nailed the passions and desires of their sinful nature to his cross and crucified them there. Pages 17 & 18

Genesis 2:7 Then the Lord God formed the man from the dust of the ground. He breathed the breath of life into the man's nostrils, and the man became a living person. Page 24

Genesis 2:8-9 Then the LORD God planted a garden in Eden in the east, and there he placed the man he had made. The LORD God made all sorts of trees grow up from the ground — trees that were beautiful and that produced delicious fruit. In the middle of the garden he placed the tree of life and the tree of the knowledge of good and evil. Page 6

Genesis 2:16-17 But the LORD God warned him, "You may freely eat the fruit of every tree in the garden — except the tree of the knowledge of good and evil. If you eat its fruit, you are sure to die." Page 6

Genesis 3:2-6 "Of course we may eat fruit from the trees in the garden," the woman replied. "It's only the fruit from the tree in the middle of the garden that we are not allowed to eat. God said, 'You must not eat it or even touch it; if you do, you will die.'" "You won't die!" the serpent replied to the woman. "God knows that your eyes will be opened as soon as you eat it, and you will be like God, knowing both good and evil." The woman was convinced. She saw that the tree was beautiful and its fruit looked delicious, and she wanted the wisdom it would give her. So she took some of the fruit and ate it. Then she gave some to her husband, who was with her, and he ate it, too. Page 6

Genesis 3:23 So the LORD God banished them from the Garden of Eden, and he sent Adam out to cultivate the ground from which he had been made. Page 6

Hebrews 1:3 The Son radiates God's own glory and expresses the very character of God, and he sustains everything by the mighty power of his command. When he had cleansed us from our sins, he sat down in the place of honor at the right hand of the majestic God in heaven. Pages 1 & 2 & 5

Hebrews 2:11-17 So now Jesus and the ones he makes holy have the same Father. That is why Jesus is not ashamed to call them his brothers and sisters. For he said to God, "I will proclaim your name to my brothers and sisters. I will praise you among your assembled people." He also said, "I will put my trust in him," that is, "I and the children God has given me." Because God's children are human beings — made of flesh and blood — the Son also became flesh and blood. For only as a human being could he die, and only by dying could he break the power of the devil, who had the power of death. Only in this way could he set free all who have lived their lives as slaves to the fear of dying. We also know that the Son did not come to help angels; he came to help the descendants of Abraham. Therefore, it was necessary for him to be made in every respect like us, his brothers and sisters, so that he could be our merciful and faithful High Priest before God. Then he could offer a sacrifice that would take away the sins of the people. Pages 1 & 2 & 20

Hebrews 2:14-15 Because God's children are human beings — made of flesh and blood — the Son also became flesh and blood. For only as a human being could he die, and only by dying could he break the power of the devil, who had the power of death. Only in this way could he set free all who have lived their lives as slaves to the fear of dying. Page 4

Hebrews 4:3 For only we who believe can enter his rest. As for the others, God said, "In my anger I took an oath: 'They will never enter my place of rest,'" even though this rest has been ready since he made the world. Page 13

Hebrews 4:7 So God set another time for entering his rest, and that time is today. God announced this through David much later in the words already quoted: "Today when you hear his voice, don't harden your hearts." Page 13

Hebrews 4:12 For the word of God is alive and powerful. It is sharper than the sharpest two-edged sword, cutting between soul and spirit, between joint and marrow. It exposes our innermost thoughts and desires. Page 24 & 26

Hebrews 9:22 With his own blood — not the blood of goats and calves — he entered the Most Holy Place once for all time and secured our redemption forever. Page 4

James 5:16 Confess your sins to each other and pray for each other so that you may be healed. The earnest prayer of a righteous person has great power and produces wonderful results. Page 26

John 1:14 So the Word became human and made his home among us. He was full of unfailing love and faithfulness. And we have seen his glory, the glory of the Father's one and only Son. Pages 1 & 2

John 3:6 Humans can reproduce only human life, but the Holy Spirit gives birth to spiritual life. Pages 19 & 24

John 3:16 For God loved the world so much that he gave his one and only Son, so that everyone who believes in him will not perish but have eternal life. Page 12

John 9:25 "I don't know whether he is a sinner," the man replied. "But I know this: I was blind, and now I can see!" Page 36

John 10:10 The thief's purpose is to steal and kill and destroy. My purpose is to give them a rich and satisfying life. Page 9

John 10:30 The Father and I are one. Pages 1 & 2

John 11:25-26 Jesus told her, "I am the resurrection and the life. Anyone who believes in me will live, even after dying. Everyone who lives in me and believes in me will never ever die. Do you believe this, Martha?" Pages 15 & 16 & 19

John 12:17 Many in the crowd had seen Jesus call Lazarus from the tomb, raising him from the dead, and they were telling others about it. Page 36

John 14:6-7 Jesus told him, "I am the way, the truth, and the life. No one can come to the Father except through me. If you had really known me, you would know who my Father is. From now on, you do know him and have seen him!" Pages 13 & 15 & 16

John 14:13-14 You can ask for anything in my name, and I will do it, so that the Son can bring glory to the Father. Yes, ask me for anything in my name, and I will do it! Page 26

John 14:20 When I am raised to life again, you will know that I am in my Father, and you are in me, and I am in you. Pages 18 & 19

John 15:7 But if you remain in me and my words remain in you, you may ask for anything you want, and it will be granted! Page 26

John 15:16 You didn't choose me. I chose you. I appointed you to go and produce lasting fruit, so that the Father will give you whatever you ask for, using my name. Page 40

John 16:28 Yes, I came from the Father into the world, and now I will leave the world and return to the Father. Page 5

John 16:33 I have told you all this so that you may have peace in me. Here on earth you will have many trials and sorrows. But take heart, because I have overcome the world. Page 10

1 John 1:7 But if we are living in the light, as God is in the light, then we have fellowship with each other, and the blood of Jesus, his Son, cleanses us from all sin. Page 4

1 John 1:9 But if we confess our sins to him, he is faithful and just to forgive us our sins and to cleanse us from all wickedness. Page 26

1 John 3:1-3 See how very much our Father loves us, for he calls us his children, and that is what we are! But the people who belong to this world don't recognize that we are God's children because they don't know him. Dear friends, we are already God's children, but he has not yet shown us what we will be like when Christ appears. But we do know that we will be like him, for we will see him as he really is. And all who have this eager expectation will keep themselves pure, just as he is pure. Page 25

1 John 3:9-10 Those who have been born into God's family do not make a practice of sinning, because God's life is in them. So they can't keep on sinning, because they are children of God.

So now we can tell who are children of God and who are children of the devil. Anyone who does not live righteously and does not love other believers does not belong to God. Page 25

1 John 5:12-13 Whoever has the Son has life; whoever does not have God's Son does not have life. I have written this to you who believe in the name of the Son of God, so that you may know you have eternal life. Pages 15 & 16

1 John 5:18-19 We know that God's children do not make a practice of sinning, for God's Son holds them securely, and the evil one cannot touch them. We know that we are children of God and that the world around us is under the control of the evil one. Page 17

Joshua 1:8 Study this Book of Instruction continually. Meditate on it day and night so you will be sure to obey everything written in it. Only then will you prosper and succeed in all you do. Page 26

Luke 1:78-79 Because of God's tender mercy, the morning light from heaven is about to break upon us, to give light to those who sit in darkness and in the shadow of death, and to guide us to the path of peace. Page 10

Luke 2:40 There the child grew up healthy and strong. He was filled with wisdom, and God's favor was on him. Page 3

Luke 2:41-47 Every year Jesus' parents went to Jerusalem for the Passover festival. When Jesus was twelve years old, they attended the festival as usual. After the celebration was over, they started home to Nazareth, but Jesus stayed behind in Jerusalem. His parents didn't miss him at first, because they assumed he was among the other travelers. But when he didn't show up that evening, they started looking for him among their relatives and friends. When they couldn't find him, they went back to Jerusalem to search for him there. Three days later they finally discovered him in the Temple, sitting among the religious teachers, listening to them and asking questions. All who heard him were amazed at his understanding and his answers. Page. 3

Luke 2:52 Jesus grew in wisdom and in stature and in favor with God and all the people. Page 3

Luke 9:60 But Jesus told him, "Let the spiritually dead bury their own dead. Your duty is to go and preach about the kingdom of God." Page 40

Luke 10:2 These were his instructions to them, "The harvest is great, but the workers are few. So pray to the Lord who is in charge of the harvest, ask him to send more workers into his fields." Page 40

Luke 19:10 For the Son of Man came to seek and save those who are lost. Page 40

Luke 24:1-7 But very early on Sunday morning the women went to the tomb, taking the spices they had prepared. They found that the stone had been rolled away from the entrance. So they went in, but they didn't find the body of the Lord Jesus. As they stood there puzzled, two men suddenly appeared to them, clothed in dazzling robes. The women were terrified and bowed with their faces to the ground. Then the men asked, "Why are you looking among the dead for someone who is alive? He isn't here! He is risen from the dead! Remember what he told you back in Galilee, that the Son of Man must be betrayed into the hands of sinful men and be crucified, and that he would rise again on the third day." Page 5

Luke 24:50-51 Then Jesus led them to Bethany, and lifting his hands to heaven, he blessed them. While he was blessing them, he left them and was taken up to heaven. Page 5

Mark 6:2-3 The next Sabbath he began teaching in the synagogue, and many who heard him were amazed. They asked, "Where did he get all this wisdom and the power to perform such miracles?" Then they scoffed, "He's just a carpenter, the son of Mary and the brother of James, Joseph, Judas, and Simon. And his sisters live right here among us." They were deeply offended and refused to believe in him. Page 3

Matthew 1:20b-23 "For the child within her was conceived by the Holy Spirit. And she will have a son, and you are to name him Jesus, for he will save his people from their sins." All of this occurred to fulfill the Lord's message through his prophet: "Look! The virgin will conceive a child! She will give birth to a son, and they will call him Immanuel, which means 'God is with us.'" Page 1

Matthew 3:13-17 Then Jesus went from Galilee to the Jordan River to be baptized by John. But John tried to talk him out of it. "I am the one who needs to be baptized by you," he said, "so why are you coming to me?" But Jesus said, "It should be done, for we must carry out all that God requires." So John agreed to baptize him. After his baptism, as Jesus came up out of the water, the heavens were opened and he saw the Spirit of God descending like a dove and settling on him. And a voice from heaven said, "This is my dearly loved Son, who brings me great joy" Pages 3 & 26

Matthew 4:19-20 Jesus called out to them, "Come, follow me, and I will show you how to fish for people!" And they left their nets at once and followed him. Page 40

Matthew 7:7-8 "Keep on asking, and you will receive what you ask for. Keep on seeking, and you will find. Keep on knocking, and the door will be opened to you. For everyone who asks, receives. Everyone who seeks, finds. And to everyone who knocks, the door will be opened. Page 26

Matthew 7:13-14 "You can enter God's Kingdom only through the narrow gate. The highway to hell is broad, and its gate is wide for the many who choose that way. But the gateway to life is very narrow and the road is difficult, and only a few ever find it. Page 23

Matthew 7:28-29 When Jesus had finished saying these things, the crowds were amazed at his teaching, for he taught with real authority — quite unlike their teachers of religious law. Page 3

Matthew 10:32 Everyone who acknowledges me publicly here on earth, I will also acknowledge before my Father in heaven. Page 40

Matthew 26:28-29 for this is my blood, which confirms the covenant between God and his people. It is poured out as a sacrifice to forgive the sins of many. Mark my words — I will not drink wine again until the day I drink it new with you in my Father's Kingdom. Page 4

Matthew 27:57-61 As evening approached, Joseph, a rich man from Arimathea who had become a follower of Jesus, went to Pilate and asked for Jesus' body. And Pilate issued an order to release it to him. Joseph took the body and wrapped it in a long sheet of clean linen cloth. He placed it in his own new tomb, which had been carved out of the rock. Then he rolled a great stone across the entrance and left. Both Mary Magdalene and the other Mary were sitting across from the tomb and watching. Page 4

1 Peter 1:18-19 For you know that God paid a ransom to save you from the empty life you inherited from your ancestors. And the ransom he paid was not mere gold or silver. It was the precious blood of Christ, the sinless, spotless Lamb of God. Page 25

1 Peter 2:24 He personally carried our sins in his body on the cross so that we can be dead to sin and live for what is right. By his wounds you are healed. Page 4

1 Peter 3:15 Instead, you must worship Christ as Lord of your life. And if someone asks you about your Christian hope, always be ready to explain it. Page 36

1 Peter 3:18 Christ suffered for our sins once for all time. He never sinned, but he died for sinners to bring you safely home to God. He suffered physical death, but he was raised to life in the Spirit. Page 12

Philippians 2:5-8 You must have the same attitude that Christ Jesus had. Though he was God, he did not think of equality with God as something to cling to. Instead, he gave up his divine privileges; he took the humble position of a slave and was born as a human being. When he appeared in human form, he humbled himself in obedience to God and died a criminal's death on a cross. Pages 1 & 2 & 22 & 25

Philippians 3:20 But we are citizens of heaven, where the Lord Jesus Christ lives. And we are eagerly waiting for him to return as our Savior. Pages 20 & 22 & 23

Philippians 4:6-7 Don't worry about anything; instead, pray about everything. Tell God what you need, and thank him for all he has done. Then you will experience God's peace, which exceeds anything we can understand. His peace will guard your hearts and minds as you live in Christ Jesus. Page 26

Proverbs 14:12 There is a path before each person that seems right, but it ends in death. Page 11

Psalm 16:11 You will show me the way of life, granting me the joy of your presence and the pleasures of living with you forever. Page 20

Psalm 40:3 He has given me a new song to sing, a hymn of praise to our God. Many will see what he has done and be amazed. They will put their trust in the Lord. Page 36

Revelation 3:20 "Look! I stand at the door and knock. If you hear my voice and open the door

I will come in, and we will share a meal together as friends. Page 9

Revelation 12:11 And they have defeated him by the blood of the lamb and by their testimony Page 36

Revelation 19:10 Then I fell down at his feet to worship him, but he said, "No, don't worship me, I am a servant God, just like you and your brothers and sisters who testify about their faith in Jesus. Worship only God. For the essence of prophecy is to give a clear witness for Jesus." Page 36

Revelation 21:2 And I saw the holy city, the new Jerusalem, coming down from God out of heaven like a bride beautifully dressed for her husband. Page 20

Romans 3:23 For everyone has sinned; we all fall short of God's glorious standard. Pages 7 & 11

Romans 5:1-2 Therefore, since we have been made right in God's sight by faith, we have peace with God because of what Jesus Christ our Lord has done for us. Because of our faith, Christ has brought us into this place of undeserved privilege where we now stand, and we confidently and joyfully look forward to sharing God's glory Pages 10 & 12

Romans 5:5 And this hope will not lead to disappointment. For we know how dearly God loves us, because he has given us the Holy Spirit to fill our hearts with his love. Page 19

Romans 5:6 When we were utterly helpless, Christ came at just the right time and died for us sinners. Page. 4

Romans 5:9 And since we have been made right in God's sight by the blood of Christ, he will certainly save us from God's condemnation. Page 8

Romans 5:11 So now we can rejoice in our wonderful new relationship with God because our Lord Jesus Christ has made us friends of God. Page 20

Romans 5:12 When Adam sinned, sin entered the world. Adam's sin brought death, so death spread to everyone, for everyone sinned. Page 7

Romans 5:18-19 Yes, Adam's one sin brings condemnation for everyone, but Christ's one act of righteousness brings a right relationship with God and new life for everyone. Because one person disobeyed God, many became sinners. But because one other person obeyed God, many will be made righteous. Pages 7 & 17

Romans 6:4-6 For we died and were buried with Christ by baptism. And just as Christ was raised from the dead by the glorious power of the Father, now we also may live new lives. Since we have been united with him in his death, we will also be raised to life as he was. We know that our old sinful selves were crucified with Christ so that sin might lose its power in our lives. We are no longer slaves to sin. Pages 18 & 19

Romans 6:11-13 So you also should consider yourselves to be dead to the power of sin and alive to God through Christ Jesus. Do not let sin control the way you live; do not give in to sinful desires. Do not let any part of your body become an instrument of evil to serve sin. Instead, give yourselves completely to God, for you were dead, but now you have new life. So use your whole body as an instrument to do what is right for the glory of God. Page 25

Romans 6:16 Don't you realize that you become the slave of whatever you choose to obey? You can be a slave to sin, which leads to death, or you can choose to obey God, which leads to righteous living. Pages 9 & 23

Romans 6:21 And what was the result? You are now ashamed of the things you used to do, things that end in eternal doom. Page 9

Romans 6:23 For the wages of sin is death, but the free gift of God is eternal life through Christ Jesus our Lord. Page 11

Romans 7:14-25 So the trouble is not with the law, for it is spiritual and good. The trouble is with me, for I am all too human, a slave to sin. I don't really understand myself, for I want to do what is right, but I don't do it. Instead, I do what I hate. But if I know that what I am doing is wrong, this shows that I agree that the law is good. So I am not the one doing wrong; it is sin living in me that does it. And I know that nothing good lives in me, that is, in my sinful nature. I want to do what is right, but I can't. I want to do what is good, but I don't. I don't want to do what is wrong, but I do it anyway. But if I do what I don't want to do, I am not really the one doing wrong; it is sin living in me that does it. I have discovered this principle of really the one doing wrong; it is sin living in me that does it. I have discovered this principle of life — that when I want to do what is right, I inevitably do what is wrong. I love God's law with all my heart. But there is another power within me that is at war with my mind. This power makes me a slave to the sin that is still within me. Oh, what a miserable person I am! Who will free me from this life that is dominated by sin and death? Thank God! The answer is in Jesus Christ our Lord. So you see how it is: In my mind I really want to obey God's law, but because of my sinful nature I am a slave to sin. Page 23

Romans 8:1-2 So now there is no condemnation for those who belong to Christ Jesus. And because you belong to him, the power of the life-giving Spirit has freed you from the power of sin that leads to death. Pages 17 & 23

Romans 8:3 The law of Moses was unable to save us because of the weakness of our sinful nature. So God did what the law could not do. He sent his own Son in a body like the bodies we sinners have. And in that body God declared an end to sin's control over us by giving his Son as a sacrifice for our sins. Pages 1 & 2 & 4

Romans 8:5-6 Those who are dominated by the sinful nature think about sinful things, but those who are controlled by the Holy Spirit think about things that please the Spirit. So letting your sinful nature control your mind leads to death. But letting the Spirit control your mind leads to life and peace. Pages 10 & 22

Romans 8:10 And Christ lives within you, so even though your body will die because of sin, the Spirit gives you life because you have been made right with God. Pages 19 & 24 & 25

Romans 8:15-17a So you have not received a spirit that makes you fearful slaves. Instead, you received God's Spirit when he adopted you as his own children. Now we call him, "Abba, Father." For his Spirit joins with our spirit to affirm that we are God's children. And since we are his children, we are his heirs. In fact, together with Christ we are heirs of God's glory. Pages 20 & 21

Romans 8:37 No, despite all these things, overwhelming victory is ours through Christ, who loved us. Page 9

Romans 10:9 If you confess with your mouth that Jesus is Lord and believe in your heart that God raised him from the dead, you will be saved. Pages 15 & 16

Romans 10:13 For "Everyone who calls on the name of the LORD will be saved." Pages 15 & 16

Romans 12:1 And so, dear brothers and sisters, I plead with you to give your bodies to God because of all he has done for you. Let them be a living and holy sacrifice — the kind he will find acceptable. This is truly the way to worship him. Page 25

Romans 12:4-5 Just as our bodies have many parts and each part has a special function, so it is with Christ's body. We are many parts of one body, and we all belong to each other. Page 25

1 Thessalonians 1:6-8 So you received the message with joy from the Holy Spirit in spite of the severe suffering it brought you. In this way, you imitated both us and the Lord. As a result, you have become an example to all the believers in Greece — throughout both Macedonia and Achaia. And now the word of the Lord is ringing out from you to people everywhere, even beyond Macedonia and Achaia, for wherever we go we find people telling us about your faith in God. Page 36

1 Thessalonians 5:23-24 Now may the God of peace make you holy in every way, and may your whole spirit and soul and body be kept blameless until our Lord Jesus Christ comes again. God will make this happen, for he who calls you is faithful. Page 24 & 25

1 Timothy 2:3-4 This is good and pleases God our Savior, who wants everyone to be saved and to understand the truth. Page 40

1 Timothy 2:5-6 For there is only one God and one Mediator who can reconcile God and humanity — the man Christ Jesus. He gave his life to purchase freedom for everyone. This is the message God gave to the world at just the right time. Pages 8 & 12

2 Timothy 1:7 For God has not given us a spirit of fear and timidity, but of power, love, and self-discipline. Page 21

Additional Resources that can be purchased on Amazon or Christian book stores.

- The Rest of the Gospel, Dan Stone and David Gregory
- Classic Christianity, Bob George
- Handbook to Happiness, Charles Solomon
- Ins and Out of Rejection, Charles Solomon
- Lifetime Guarantee, Bill Gillham
- The Normal Christian Life, Watchman Nee
- Sit Walk Stand, Watchman Nee
- Release of the Spirit, Watchman Nee
- Birthright, David Needham
- The True Vine, Andrew Murray
- Abide in Christ, Andrew Murray
- Absolute Surrender, Andrew Murray
- Victory in Christ, Charles Trumbull
- The Key to Triumphant Living, Jack Taylor
- The Saving Life of Christ, W. Ian Thomas
- The Gift of Forgiveness, Charles Stanley
- The Blessing of Brokenness, Charles Stanley
- Adversity, Charles Stanley
- Truefaced, John Lynch
- My Utmost for His Highest (Devotional), Oswald Chambers
- Forgiven Forever, Bob George
- The Grace Awakening, Charles Swindoll
- The Sufficiency of Christ, John MacArther
- Hudson Taylor's Spiritual Secret, Dr. and Mrs. Howard Taylor
- Weekly e-devotional GraceNotes, John Woodward. Available through www.GraceNotebook.com
- For Me to Live is Christ, Group study course, Charles Solomon
- The Cross, Your Victory Today, CD Series by Dr. Charles Stanley (and many other sermons by Dr. Stanley)
- The Shackling of Grace, Lee LeFebre
- The Exchanged Life Conference, CD Series by Lee LeFebre
- Free at Last, Tony Evans
- Dr. Tony Evans (most sermons)
- Gregory Dickow (most sermons)
- Romans: Chapters 5-8, Any Version of the Bible
- www.gracefellowshipintl.com
- www.thelifebookstore.com
- Seeking God through Prayer & Meditation, David Howell
- Fully Alive and Finally Free, David Howell

Prison Book Project
PO Box 592
Titusville, FL 32781